GW01316265

THE ACCEPTABLE PRESSURE GROUP
Inequality in the penal lobby: a case study of the Howard League and RAP

THE ACCEPTABLE PRESSURE GROUP

Inequality in the penal lobby: a case study of the Howard League and RAP

MICK RYAN
Thames Polytechnic

Published by

Saxon House, Teakfield Limited,
Westmead, Farnborough, Hants., England

ISBN 0 566 00163 2

Printed in Great Britain by David Green (Printers) Ltd, Kettering, Northamptonshire.

Contents

Acknowledgements vi

Abbreviations vii

1 Introduction 1

2 Pluralism 6

3 The Howard Association and the Howard League: a synoptic appreciation 1866–1976 28

4 The Howard League: a conventional and a radical critique 75

5 Radical Alternatives to Prison 99

6 Conclusion 151

Select Bibliography 159

Index 161

Acknowledgements

When I first decided to write a book on the penal lobby the Howard League gave me access to the minutes of its Executive Committee. The minutes of this committee, which was later replaced by a governing council, turned out to be very informative, and I am happy to place on record my thanks to the League for its generous cooperation. Naturally, members of the League will be more than a little anxious about the political way in which their work has been interpreted. This is understandable, but the more I came to grips with what Radical Alternatives to Prison (RAP) was really saying the more that perspective became inevitable, even though it was not the perspective with which I had started out.

To the Director of the Howard League, Martin Wright, I am especially grateful. He answered my many enquiries with characteristic thoroughness, and in argument was always tough-minded in defence of the League. It will become clear that I am also very much indebted to a former member of the Howard League's Executive Committee, Dr Gordon Rose. His history of the League is, in its own terms at least, authoritative, and I have relied on it a good deal for the first part of chapter 3. I recall too, late in 1976, a long and interesting conversation on the penal lobby with the League's present chairman, Louis Blom-Cooper.

RAP's attitude towards my work was very open, and I cannot recall being denied permission to look at any document that was available at Eastbourne House. There are documentary gaps here and there, but nothing crucial. Between 1975 and 1977 Eastbourne House in London's East End was a good place to visit, and I am truly thankful to RAP's office staff, Gail Coles, Liz Middleton and Betty Potts for all their help and encouragement. To Ros Kane, my thanks for a long and revealing interview at the Newham Alternative Project in the summer of 1975. With Mike Fitzgerald (PROP) and Victoria Greenwood, who once worked for RAP as a member of its full time staff, I also had the chance to exchange ideas.

The librarians at Thames Polytechnic were extremely helpful over my research, particularly Imogen Forster.

Finally, my wife is a social scientist herself, and her intellectual contribution to this book, as my close colleagues will guess, has been considerable.

Abbreviations

CUAG	Control Units Action Group
HLPR	Howard League for Penal Reform
ISTD	Institute for the Study and Treatment of Delinquency
KRIM	The Association for a Humane Criminal Policy (Denmark)
NACRO	National Association for the Care and Resettlement of Offenders
NAP	Newham Alternatives Project
NAPO	National Association of Probation Officers
NCCL	National Council for Civil Liberties
NDC	National Deviancy Conference
NMAG	NAPO Members' Action Group
PMRC	Prison Medical Reform Council
RAP	Radical Alternatives to Prison
PROP	Preservation of the Rights of Prisoners
PUSSI	Prostitutes United for Sexual and Social Integration

1 Introduction

Students of politics who study a particular pressure group or a particular lobby need to justify this undertaking since the pressure group universe has been visited many times before and as a consequence a whole range of theoretical constructs seems readily available. Indeed, it might appear that the function of pressure groups and their operation within the British political system has been so authoritatively detailed by scholars on both sides of the Atlantic that further work in this field is unnecessary; to add yet another case study to an already long list would contribute little or nothing to our understanding of how the political system really works. To demonstrate that this view is not tenable is the first task, and not least because its survival would guarantee that pressure group studies retain what has been their traditional bias, that is, an almost exclusive concern with the powerful, those groups whose legitimacy is unquestioned and where access to those who determine public policy is regular and easy. But what about the less powerful, those groups whose legitimacy is doubted? In an allegedly free, plural society, in which groups are actively encouraged to form and press their views on government, how is it that such groups are almost defined out of the political system altogether? We assume that there would not be much disagreement over the claim that this question has received very little attention from serious students of the pressure group universe. Indeed, in Britain at least, the classification of pressure groups has been devised in such a way as to actually obscure the fact that there are groups whose legitimacy is in doubt, whose credentials do push them to the edge of the policy making process. Further, to the extent that such groups acquire their outsider status by virtue of their ideological predispositions, then the existing classification clearly ignores that pluralism has its own well-defined ideological limits.

The purpose of this book is the exact opposite, that is, it attempts to both illustrate and emphasise the limits of pluralism, to bring home to the student of politics, through a detailed study of the penal lobby, how governments discriminate against radical pressure groups in favour of liberal or conservative groups whose views imply no fundamental critique of the existing economic and political order. The penal lobby provides a clear example of this pattern of discrimination at work, not least because in this field fundamental questions about the legitimacy of the state, the freedom of the individual versus the needs of society, are endemic.

During the last few years the penal lobby has received more than its fair share of attention. In particular, much has been made of its call for a decisive shift in the direction of penal policy away from imprisonment. Although some sections of the public have found this demand too permissive successive home secretaries have been persuaded to introduce legislation aimed specifically at keeping offenders out of prison, or, as in the case of parole, ensuring their early release. Why this should be so is not hard to understand. In the first place prison is expensive. To keep an adult male offender incarcerated for a week costs the Exchequer in the region of £80 and this does not include the cost of maintaining his family on social security. Secondly, and more decisive in the long run, there is very little evidence to suggest that imprisonment contributes towards rehabilitation. Indeed, quite the opposite seems to be true since the more time an offender spends in prison the more likely he is to return there to suffer further alienation from his family and the community. Moreover, the prison experience is essentially brutalising as the widespread prison riots of 1972 and the setting up of the Movement for the Preservation of the Rights of Prisoners (PROP) confirm. In an attempt to move away from this expensive, ineffectual and harsh system, and to reduce the growing pressure on Britain's overcrowded prisons, the Home Office cautiously began to experiment with community-based correctives for certain types of offender. Although it is important to remain open-minded about these experiments – some have demonstrably failed through inadequate funding while others have yet to be fully tried – the policy move away from imprisonment has been generally welcomed by those pressure groups which together make up the penal lobby. As strange as it may seem, perhaps the one qualified exception to this, the one pressure group which is highly ambivalent about the provision of alternatives is Radical Alternatives to Prison (RAP), a group whose basic assumptions seem to imply a fundamental critique of the existing economic and political order and the manner in which we chose to define and correct deviant behaviour. It is on the exact nature of these assumptions that we wish to focus and the way in which they differ from the assumptions of other groups in the penal lobby and, in particular, the Howard League for Penal Reform.

The Howard League, established in the 1860s, takes its name from John Howard, the high sheriff of Bedfordshire who performed the very valuable task of collecting and publishing a complete range of sensational data on the state of prisons in England and Wales in the eighteenth century. The League is consistent in its praise of Howard's reliance on 'the facts' and consciously emphasises the same empirical tradition. During the first fifty years of its existence the League had little to boast about. Indeed, it might have faded into total obscurity had it not been for the outbreak of the First World War which led to the imprisonment of a number of middle class conscientious objectors who were so appalled by the brutality of the prison system that they were more than willing to add their voices to the growing chorus for reform. This was eventually to work to the Howard League's advantage, thanks mainly to the efforts of Margery Fry, and in the inter-war period the League emerged as a very real and dominant force in the long struggle for penal reform. This pre-eminence continued until well into the 1960s and even though the penal lobby is now more competitive than in the past the Howard League still occupies a special place. In 1975 it had a membership of around 1,300. Many of its rank and file members are magistrates, probation officers, social workers, all solid middle class professionals who have direct contact with the penal system. Until recently at least two-thirds of the League's members lived in London and the south east, and most of these lived in London itself. As the League's membership is highly centralised so is its policy making. There is only a handful of local and regional branches and the overall responsibility for the League's policy rests firmly with its Council and Executive Committee, many of whose members are London based with established connections in Whitehall. This highly centralised style of operating is, it should be stressed, very much in the League's tradition. Taking over from the great Margery Fry the League's officials operate as a small, well connected knot of reformers whose contact with those people who operate the levers of power is perhaps closer than with their own passive membership. To suggest that the League has easy access to Whitehall, and that it is listened to by those who are responsible for devising penal policy, is not meant to imply that the League is always in agreement with official policy. This is clearly not the case. However, such an easy relationship does imply that there are no fundamental disagreements between the Home Office and the Howard League and it is this underlying agreement which gives the League its position of considerable advantage, which a pressure group like Radical Alternatives to Prison can never hope to achieve unless it is prepared to modify the nature of its political critique.

Radical Alternatives to Prison was established in 1970. It was set up to replace the Prison Reform Council which, after its brief revival in defence of imprisoned nuclear disarmers in the 1960s, was all but moribund. Like the Howard League RAP is essentially London based, but though it has its probation officers, lawyers and social workers, its membership of around 300 is younger and altogether less a part of the legal and welfare establishment. RAP has always been organised on a fairly loose rein. When it first got started policy was the responsibility of the Nucleus, a small group of up to a dozen or so keen members who ran the group's headquarters in East London. This arrangement was democratic to the extent that a member got on to the Nucleus by simply 'being around and being active'. Although this attempt to do away with the 'bourgeois apparatus' of elections was not entirely successful, and a more formally constituted policy committee was set up in 1976, RAP has no wish to 'dictate to its members' and local branches where they exist are virtually autonomous.

The decision to establish a policy committee was partly an attempt to salvage RAP's link with its longstanding sponsor Christian Action. Formed after the last war by Canon John Collins, Christian Action is a registered charity which is run, in theory at least, by a council of busy worthies like Lord Longford. RAP's relationship with Christian Action has never been an easy one. Some of RAP's members object to being labelled, if only by association, as christian while others resent what they see as occasional attempts by the Council to interfere in RAP's internal affairs. Another real difficulty, perhaps the decisive difficulty, is RAP's political perspective on penal policy. This not only causes Christian Action considerable embarrassment, it also sets RAP apart from more established groups in the penal lobby, in particular the Howard League, and at the same time keeps it very much at the edge of the policy making process.

RAP's attitude towards penal policy is determined by wider considerations relating to the law making process. According to much of RAP's literature criminal law serves not the interests of the community as a whole but the interests of a powerful class or powerful groups. The criminal law, in fact, is used as a legitimate force to suppress the interests of the majority in favour of the economically or socially powerful few. This is unacceptable to RAP, and to the extent that this judgement predicates its interpretation of penal policy then RAP is inclined to view any suggested reforms as merely ways of reinforcing an economic and political system of which it is highly critical. Not surprisingly, RAP is viewed by those who administer penal policy as carrying a foreign and politically hostile message. The Howard League is in an altogether different position. It does not challenge the legitimacy of the criminal law which it somehow views as the expression of a broadly based consensus. Its emphasis, therefore, has traditionally been to uphold the law, arguing only for more humane and effective ways of treating those offenders who, through 'illness' or irresponsible behaviour, have chosen to ignore it. This puts the Howard League on the inside track, making it, argues RAP, a force for the defence of the powerful. No wonder the Howard League is an 'approved' group and that it has regular and easy access to those who determine penal policy.

When the Home Office finally appeared to have grasped that even in its own terms imprisonment was a fairly futile punishment, it looked as if the search for alternatives might be given priority. In the debates which followed, in the various arguments which were to surround issues like community service and the recommendations of the Younger Report, the ideological rift sketched out above was to divide RAP from the Howard League, and central government agencies like the probation service were instrumental in emphasising that rift. Given its radical assumptions RAP faced some tough strategic choices. These were not always wisely made and RAP came close to being defined out of the policy process altogether. That this could still happen is a challenge to those liberal democrats who boast about the tolerance of pluralism rather than acknowledging its limits.

2 Pluralism

Most Western liberal democracies emphasise the value of social and political diversity. A plural Western society in which all groups can freely organise and compete in the policy making process is thought of as highly desirable. Certainly it is more desirable than totalitarian societies, left or right, which visibly and often ruthlessly suppress dissident groups whether political, cultural, ethnic or religious. For Western liberal democrats the very nature of political rule is defined in the context of this diversity since politics is about the peaceful conciliation of conflicting group interests:

> Politics arises from accepting the fact of the simultaneous existence of different groups, hence different interests and different traditions, within a territorial unit under a common rule . . . The political method of rule is to listen to these . . . groups so as to conciliate them as far as possible and give them a legal position, a sense of security, some clear and reasonably safe means of articulation, by which these . . . groups can and will speak freely.[1]

This emphasis on political rule as the conciliation of group diversity as opposed to individual diversity is common to much political analysis in the twentieth century and to some extent at least it reflects the influence of the founder of the American tradition of analytic pluralism, Arthur Fisher Bentley, whose seminal work *The Process of Government* first appeared in 1908. Bentley had little time for the idea of the individual as a concept for use in political analysis. He could see no point in carrying on political analysis as if everyone lived in a small and intimate city-state where the individual related directly and personally to the central authority in that state. This is just no longer true; the relationship between the individual and the state is now defined by a host of intermediate groups and if the student of politics wants to get to grips with the way the political process really works then he needs a new organising concept, namely, the idea of the group.

Bentley's scientific pretentions, his belief that all that really mattered in the study of politics, including ideas, could be defined as group activity and duly quantified need not detain us here, but of relevant interest is that his theory was close enough to description to sustain a whole range of empirical enquiries into the American group universe. Peter Odegard's *Pressure Politics: The Story of the Anti-Saloon League* appeared in 1928. A year later Pendleton Herring produced his pioneering work on *Group Representation Before Congress.* Other important works followed from Harewood Childs, *Labour and Capital in National Politics* (1930), Louise Rutherford's *The Influence of the American Bar Association on Public Opinion and Legislation* (1937) and Donald C. Blaisdell's *Economic Power and Political Pressures* (1941). More pressure group studies appeared after the war and by 1950 one distinguished American academic was to argue that *The Process of Government* had surely acquired the status of being one of the most important books on government ever to be published in any country. [2]

Even if such praise is thought to be generous it is difficult not to concede that Bentley's emphasis on groups helped some way towards updating political analysis and identifying what is now called the group basis of politics which, in its turn, is the foundation on which modern pluralists build their polemic. However, it is important to grasp that Bentley's commitment to groups, his conceptualisation of politics as the clash of group interests, rested on an unstated assumption, namely, the existence of an ideological consensus. To the extent that politics is about the play-off between rival groups, the conciliation of opposing interest, sharply conflicting ideologies cannot produce the goods. As closed systems of thought contending ideologies will not meet, the basis for a lasting compromise is lost. [3] It is significant that Bentley, a mature citizen in a federal policy, could conceive of politics as the simple clash of group interests, a process which was almost Newtonian in operation and therefore amenable to scientific measurement. Bentley's context has been aptly summarised by Bernard Crick:

> By the 1900s the unity of American experience and the stress on tactical considerations of politics in a federal system gave a meaning to politics that was radically unlike the ideological and doctrinal struggles of Europe. Progressive reformers might still try to hold fast to the ultra-individualism of direct democracy, but the new practical scientists began to see politics as a contest for marginal privilege by a great many pressure groups, mostly regional and economic rather than primarily ideological and doctrinal. To the student these could all appear as very much equal in their claims. They all operated broadly within the same assumptions of the one liberal democratic tradition. They make it easy for the student of politics to see himself as just the

dispassionate observer of the democratic plurality of pressure groups. There was only the need for the methodological discussion of how best to study these groups and for the *primum mobile* of the system to be seen as 'power' or 'interest'. There was felt to be no need for the kind of critical recourse to philosophy and history that the European student of politics had to make. [4]

It is sometimes difficult to believe that the American context has changed that much, other than perhaps in becoming more explicit. Robert Dahl, for example, in his much praised *A Preface to Democratic Theory* comes to the conclusion that what we normally refer to as politics, the struggle between rival groups to achieve their goals, is merely the 'chaff', and that beneath and sustaining this struggle is a consensus, a broad area of basic agreement about what alternatives are acceptable and the best way to resolve disagreements when they occur. [5] Given this basic agreement students of politics can concentrate on politics as it is, to examine it as a process or a system.

From a radical point of view what the American analysts have done is to substitute a model of group conflict for class conflict. To some extent such a charge would not have unduly surprised Bentley. After all, in a specific reference to America he did claim that in practice class domination had broken down and left the way clear for a 'group approach'. [6] Of particular interest from a British point of view is that this observation roughly parallels that of another American, Samuel Beer, about British politics in the fifties, i.e. that a class interpretation of politics was giving way to a consensus in which group will and not class conflict was the most prominent feature of the political landscape. What Beer argued is worth considering in some detail.

Beer is the first to admit that the Labour Party, since its formation, has been a coalition. Its membership has always included people of widely differing political perspectives. However, to the extent that the party has ever been really together it was united in the inter-war period and immediately after 1945 when all sections of the party traced their grievances to a common source, capitalism. [7] There was no suggestion that the capitalist system could put these grievances right, that it could somehow reform itself from within. Capitalism was inherently wasteful and inefficient, it also had a corrupting influence, turning men against men in the lust for profit. There was only one remedy, the overthrow of capitalism and the introduction of the public ownership of the means of production, distribution and exchange. This goal, this ambition, argues Beer, was the very soul of the party during the 1920s and 1930s. The fact that it was to be achieved gradually and through parliament did not detract from its revolutionary nature. Further, the assault on capitalism was to be led by those who had suffered from it most, the working class. This political role gave the working class an even greater sense of identity; it built upon their separate existence as an economic class in a hierarchic society. [8]

It is clear, then, that Beer is convinced about the Labour Party's commitment to socialism and the class struggle between the wars. However, he is equally convinced that by the late 1940s this commitment was under attack, an attack which struck at the very roots of the Party's ideological commitment, Clause IV, Labour's goal to 'secure for the workers by hand or by brain the full fruits of their industry and the most equitable distribution thereof that may be possible, upon the basis of the common ownership of the means of production, distribution and exchange ...'. The details of this struggle, the confrontations between revisionist and fundamentalist, are not our immediate concern. Of crucial interest, however, is how Beer interpreted the outcome of the struggle, his belief that it reflected a growing consensus, a society in which disagreements across class lines over ideology were on the wane. Class conflict was giving way to group conflict. He commented:

> By the early 1950s Labourites and Conservatives seemed well on the way toward executing a classic movement of a two party system. From positions widely separating them on issues of substantial, even fundamental, importance they have moved markedly toward one another. Within the Labour Party ... powerful forces resisted this movement; and one could never say that British socialism had quite deserted its ancient ideological orthodoxies. Yet on the scale of left and right, as defined in British politics, each party was drifting towards the center, as the party of the left extended its appeal to groups on its right and the party of the right extended its appeal to groups on its left. Class and ideological contours faded while interest groups appeared as more prominent features of the political scene. It was against the background of these developments that R.T. McKenzie concluded in 1958 that 'pressure groups, taken together, are a far more important channel of communication than parties for the transmission of political ideas from the mass of their citizenry to their leaders'. [9]

Although this systematic interpretation did not appear in Britain until 1965, Beer had been arguing much the same thesis throughout the 1950s in academic journals like the *American Political Science Review* and the *Political Quarterly.* [10] His reliance on the American tradition of political analysis is obvious enough, even though he attempts to give it the gloss of a long historical perspective. The arrival of the consensus and group involvement with the welfare state and the managed economy made his 'new' group politics seem all the more intelligible, the facts appearing to square with the analysis, albeit in an un-American context.

The American emphasis on groups and the idea of consensus, the politics of Mr Butskill and Mr Gaitler as Beer referred to the British context, was not unrelated to the struggle between East and West, the Cold War. [11] Seymour Lipset, for example, was to argue that the consensus was a reflection of liberal democratic achievement, the fundamental problems of the industrial revolution had been solved, workers now had their place in the sun and while conservatives accepted the welfare state the democratic left had come to the salutary conclusion that 'over-all state power' is a threat to freedom. [12] Three cheers for Western liberal democracies. Groups have a vital role to play in protecting these societies from the threat of totalitarianism, or that at least is what Kornhauser asked us to believe. [13] His thesis begins with the assumption that mass politics, which in its extreme form is labelled totalitarianism, is likely to occur in the following circumstances. First, where government elites lose their exclusiveness as a result of popular participation in crucial areas of decision making (in effect, Tocqueville's warning about the tyranny of the majority). This is what Kornhauser refers to as the aristocratic fear of mass politics. Second, mass politics will occur in a society dominated by an elite capable of mobilising large numbers of isolated individuals. This is the democratic fear of mass politics. It follows, therefore, that to avoid mass politics and possible totalitarianism, society must be insulated from both these possibilities; social structures, formal and informal, must be geared to this objective, and a major insulating structure argues Kornhauser, is the group. Its functions *vis-a-vis* the aristocratic fear of politics are essentially two-fold. To start with, it must mediate between elite and masses, organising opinion and refining extreme demands. Group leaders have an important role to play in this respect, i.e. since their own authority is inextricably bound up with the existing system they are prepared to play by the rules, making only moderate demands which contribute towards stability. This interpretation as self-interest is supposedly balanced by the knowledge that group leaders genuinely hold liberal democratic values supporting free speech, tolerance and fair dealing.

Thus, groups and the shared assumptions of their leaders help to exclude the masses from having an undue influence in crucial areas of decision making. Second, the plurality of groups is also significant because it makes it more difficult for any single group to dominate .

Groups have an important function *vis-a-vis* the democratic fear of mass politics since research shows that mass movements are sustained by an autocratic elite appeal to isolated individuals:

> Social classes which provide disproportionate support for mass movements are those that possess the fewest social ties among their members. This means above all the lower social classes. However, since there are sections of all social classes which tend to be socially atomised, members of all social classes are to be found among the participants in mass politics; unattached (especially freelance) intellectuals, marginal (especially small) businessmen and farmers and isolated workers have engaged in mass politics in times of crisis.[14]

Clearly, if these socially atomised individuals can be absorbed by groups the threat of totalitarianism will lessen. Kornhauser thus succeeded in defining the group as a major structural determinant in sustaining a plural elitist democracy.

If groups were as important as Beer and Kornhauser were suggesting, then it came as something of a surprise to the British tradition of political studies, a tradition which, when it moved away from the great books of political theory, hardly went further, in most cases, than the formal features of the constitution such as the Cabinet, Parliament and the political parties. What happened beyond these formal structures was largely ignored. Thus, Beer was simply forced to ask, 'Where are your pressure groups?'[15] Initially he did not receive too many replies. The editors of *Political Quarterly* regretted that the study of pressure groups in Britain had been 'almost entirely ignored' and W.J.M. Mackenzie in the *British Journal of Sociology* could only refer to work in progress.[16] However, there was a concerted effort to put this right and between 1958 and 1964 at least nine books were published with the role of pressure groups as their focus. First in the field was S.E. Finer's classic, *Anonymous Empire: A Study of the Lobby in Great Britain.* In the same year, 1958, came J.D. Stewart's, *British Pressure Groups: Their Role in Relation to the House of Commons.* Then followed: H. Eckstein, *Pressure Group Politics; the Case of the British Medical Association* (1960); H.H. Wilson, *Pressure Group: The Campaign for Commercial Television* (1961); A. Potter, *Organised Interests in British National Politics*

(1961); G. Rose, *The Struggle for Penal Reform; The Howard League and its Predecessors* (1961) and in 1962 P. Self and H. Storing's *The State and the Farmer* and James B. Christoph's *Capital Punishment and British Politics.* At least four of these authors were American: Eckstein, Storing, Christoph and Wilson. W.J.M. Mackenzie was indeed right to stress that the British interest in the study of pressure groups was being stimulated from abroad.

On the British side there were reservations though, not least being the anxiety that we were in danger of reverting to a form of medieval corporatism in which the individual was only significant as a member of a group. To say, as Bentley did, that the individual 'stated for himself' was of no value in understanding society, was going too far. Apart from anything else it denied that individuals could influence governments and that was demonstrably false. Government as such also indicated an area of anxiety. There was a lot of agreement that the two main parties were coming together, that their programmes reflected a growing consensus, and that in the context of the welfare state and the managed economy politics would increasingly become the trade-off between rival interest groups for marginal gains. However, British students of politics could not accept the idea, implicit in the American understanding of pluralism, that government was, at worst, simply about registering a mysterious equilibrium of opposing social forces or, at best, acting as broker between conflicting pressure/interest groups. Government was much more purposeful, and even programmatic, with the public interest as its major focus. The British anxiety was well stated by Bernard Crick when he remarked about Bentley's book on *The Process of Government* that in spite of its title it contained a lot about politics and just about nothing on government.[17]

The fact that some pressure groups are more powerful than others was an obvious truth that British pluralists faced up to from the start, or that at least is what they would probably claim. S.E. Finer, for example, agreed that God was on the side of the big battalions.[18] By this Finer was not referring to wealth as such. In any case, he felt that wealth played only a small part in gaining favour. Wealthy pressure groups could not bribe government officials to give them preference over other groups, nor could they maintain private armies (!). True, they could put their resources at the disposal of one of the political parties at election time and then sit back and wait for the *quid pro quo.* But given that in the British context what can be spent by political parties on election campaigns is strictly controlled , this strategy offers very little leverage. To use resources between elections is a possibility. Wealthy groups might, for example, press their case through the media, and no doubt this does happen. But media coverage is not determined only by wealth; many financially weak groups get extensive publicity because editors happen to believe that what they are doing is newsworthy. If wealth is not an issue, what exactly does Finer mean by the 'big battalions'? He seems to be referring to 'clout', that is, some pressure groups by virtue of their role as producer groups can exert more pressure on governments than non-producer groups. Further, producer groups are not all equal in their strength. Some by virtue of their strategic role in the economy have more power, more 'clout' than others. This inequality is obvious to government and its role is to make sure that 'the less strongly organised do not go to the wall'; it must work to achieve 'some measure of distributive justice'.[19] This is government acting in the public interest, not simply registering opposing pressures, and not merely broking between Group A and Group B with no consideration for other groups.

It is clear that Finer did not see the public interest as Rousseau saw the general will, i.e. as something that was somehow antagonistic to particular wills or group interests. He took a very different view, arguing that governments are inclined to adopt a Benthamite interpretation of the public interest and set out to secure for each group what it wants to the point that this is consistent with all other groups securing what they want. Looking after the public interest in this sense is one of government's most important functions. This view admits more easily the idea that pressure groups are essentially sectional in their interest. Finer accepted this, indeed, he argued that it would be very odd if they did not spend their time badgering the government in defence of their own sectional interests. That is exactly what their members expected. On the other hand, it was significant that pressure groups frequently argued that what was in their interest was also in the nation's interest: 'What is good for General Motors is good for America'. In most cases this might not be true. It might not even be more than a token argument, but the fact that pressure groups even bother to make it indicates a generally held view that in reaching any decisions the government has a duty to consider 'the public interest'.

There remains, of course, the problem of exactly whose interests are being articulated when pressure groups make their demands on government. That is, it is not always certain that what pressure group leaders want is always what their rank and file members want. Eckstein illustrated this worry in his study of the British Medical Association.[20] The BMA found itself campaigning hard against the National Health Service only to discover (from an opinion survey) that part of its policy was not supported by the rank and file. In much larger pressure groups where there are even more full time officials than in the BMA, the chances that the 'official line' will be at variance with membership opinion are even greater. In his 1955 survey of 'what we know about pressure groups' and 'what we still need to find out', W.J.M. Mackenzie devoted a whole section of his paper to questions of internal structure.[21] He seemed particularly anxious over the problem of pressure group democracy and argued that it was important to find out just how many members of any given group were activists. Finer shared this anxiety and quoted, for example, a sample survey showing that attendance at Co-operative Society general meetings varied from 3.29 per cent to 0.04 per cent of the membership.[22] The concern expressed by Finer, Mackenzie and Eckstein contains a certain paradox since, if Kornhauser is right, then pressure group leaders are among the elite who temper the unruly masses. Thus, the fact that they might sometimes clash with their members and appear to act against their felt needs or interests is not surprising, indeed it is inevitable if a viable democracy is to survive. To be sure, the argument is not quite so simple, on the other hand, it is difficult not to believe that pressure group leaders, and trade union leaders in particular, were criticised by some academic theorists no matter what action they took.

If the idea of politics as the play-off between opposing pressure group interests had to cope with the fact that some groups were more powerful than others and that some were undemocratic, there was also the problem of the unorganised. Who was to look after their interests? The problem is a real one and can only be effectively overcome by hopeful appeals to conservative metaphysics. There is, for example, a partial solution based on the assumption that those groups with power acknowledge the potential strength of certain unorganised interests and accommodate, at least to some extent, their aspirations. That this is a way of safeguarding the *status quo,* or in Bentley's language, the existing equilibrium, is obvious enough. David B. Truman, one of Bentley's later disciples, illustrated this process at work when he quoted Key to the effect that the Delta planters of the Mississippi were willing to argue for their negroes' accommodation in matters such as health and education even though the negroes were virtually unorganised.[23] Beyond this it must be presumed that those interests whose potential organised strength is negligible can only rely on what Finer refers to variously as 'standards' or 'common beliefs'. In the British context the government can be relied upon to interpret these standards or beliefs in defence of the unorganised.

Truly, the plight of the unorganised in the pressure group universe did not much concern British academics. More relevant, it was argued, was the problem of anonymity, the feeling that what pressure groups get up to, the deals they worked out with governments and so on, were all shielded from public scrutiny, amounting to an 'Anonymous Empire'. The force of this objection was not only the very reasonable democratic concern that deals when they are made should be openly arrived at. The objection went further than this since the Anonymous Empire was to become not only one of the reasons for Parliament's decline, it was also used to explain the nation's failure, Britain's apparent inability in the 1960s to keep pace with the achievements of its neighbours, particularly those countries which together formed the European Economic Communities. If the argument was typically British, focussing as it did on the role of institutions, it was also complex. The starting point in many ways was the economy.

During the 1960s Britain suffered a good deal from inflation and a recurring deficit in the balance of payments. It was felt that a cure for these economic ailments could be found, and that the cure could be made acceptable to the majority of politicians in both major parties and, indeed, to the leaders of many trade unions and business pressure groups. However, the difficulty would come in trying to persuade the public to accept the cure. Samuel Beer made precisely this point:

> The problem is, therefore, not so much to devise economic programmes which, if they were carried out, would meet the problems. It is, rather, to win such understanding and acceptance of government programmes among the public, as individuals, and as members of producers' and consumers' groups, that they will adjust their own behaviour about the requirements of these programmes. The central problem, in short, is to win consent – and winning consent is a political problem in a political process.[24]

Although this interpretation was not without support, there were academics, notably Bernard Crick, who felt that the political process, as it then operated, was simply not capable of winning such consent. [25] On the contrary, there was a blockage in the vertical communications system, between governors and the governed, which rendered the political process almost wholly impotent in this respect. Crick pointed to Labour's Prices and Incomes legislation, arguing that it was a complex, technical piece of legislation which would affect every member of the community. To succeed it required explanation and persuasion. It received neither and therefore failed. In effect, Crick was saying that modern governments impose, whether in relation to economic problems or indeed to other areas of social activity, complex patterns of adjustment, and if the public are to consent to these adjustments their purpose must be more fully debated, explained and justified. A crucial weakness in the British political process was its failure to fulfil this educative function.

This weakness could be put right by reforming Parliament. It was argued that the vertical communications system was blocked at this point. Messages were adequately transmitted from the public to Parliament, but the same could not be said of the reverse process. This led Crick to emphasise that Parliament was not simply just an institution for representing public opinion, it was also responsible for disseminating information and in this sense educating public opinion about the policies and conduct of government. Only when this was appreciated could Parliament, and more especially the House of Commons, be transformed into an effective institution for mobilising consent. True, it was not argued that this alone would overcome the difficulties facing Britain in the 1960s, but it was made plain that without this transformation all other contributions towards a solution would fail.

The question immediately arises, what developments have taken place to render Parliament ineffective as an educative institution? Most answers centre on the fact that government's increasing intervention in social and economic affairs has been accompanied by legislation of increasing complexity. The capability of members to debate, explain and justify legislation is now much less than at any time in the past. In the nineteenth century, with the exception of certain technical industrial legislation, the subjects that Parliament had to decide on did not require much specialised knowledge. Legal, social and economic relationships and their adjustment are now immeasurably more intricate and subtle.[26] Confronted with this development, and unaided by the expertise of the administration, members are incapable of evaluating the force and rationale of government decisions. To put it bluntly, members are incapable of educating themselves about executive policies, let alone educating the public. Until this situation was remedied there was little hope that Parliament could fulfil what Crick argued to be its most important function.

Accompanying, and indeed a necessary constituent in the progress towards more complex legislation, has been the increasing use of enabling powers which confer on the administration wide discretionary authority. In an important sense the modern legislative process can be characterised as one in which Parliament concerns itself with broad authorisation, the passing of complex general rules, while the administration at a later stage fills in the more specific provisions. The significance of this development is difficult to overestimate. To begin with it has very real value in terms of flexibility. The National Farmers' Union, for example, was fond of pointing out to its members that Parliament has a very crowded timetable and if every detail of the government's intervention in agriculture was set out and embodied in statute any attempts at amendment in the light of experience or changed circumstances would take months and perhaps even years to achieve. To legislate in more general terms, to provide the framework for later adjustments as it were, was much more preferable. However, this obvious enthusiasm for enabling legislation, and the flexibility which stems from it, did not prevent the union from appreciating that this meant more power to the administration and less for Parliament. [27]

Those reformers who wanted to see Parliament restored as an educative institution saw the dangers in this trend. It was argued that many of the administrative adjustments, albeit it made legally and within the framework of existing law, were brought about by the administration as a result of consultations with the leaders of pressure groups, adjustments concluded in private and largely at the expense of Parliamentary scrutiny. John Mackintosh, for example, pointed to the National Farmers' Union as a pressure group whose relationship with the administration was often regarded as a model to be copied. He explained how the Union, making use of its role embodied in the 1947 Agricultural Act, held annual meetings with the administration to determine the level and distribution of farm subsidies for the coming year. The process, complained Mackintosh, is shrouded in complete secrecy.[28] Thus, Parliament is excluded from the entire process by which the annual review is determined. The review simply appears as government policy, a *fait accompli.* The weakness inherent in this process of decision making is obvious enough. To paraphrase Samuel Beer, it is not reasonable to identify with the output of the government process when only the product and not the process is actually revealed, for the very simple reason that the policy process itself examines a whole range of potential policies. Only when this is revealed is it possible to judge whether or not the government's decision is the right one. To expect members of Parliament to educate the public, to somehow mobilise consent when they are not in any position to make such a judgement is expecting too much. Democracy requires that the policy process and, in particular, the dialogue between pressure groups and the administration be opened up to Parliamentary scrutiny.

It could be argued that the annual price review is perhaps a bad example for the reformers to have chosen since the normal pattern of adjustment between pressure groups and the administration involves relatively uncontroversial issues. There is some truth in this observation, but it cannot be denied that the relationship between pressure groups and the administration is highly developed and largely closed. As Finer has commented, there is a vast body of business transacted and much of it never makes a mark in Parliament or the Press. [29] It is now almost taken for granted that if a pressure group wants something it goes to the administration first; and even if it returns empty handed, there are constraints on an approach to Parliament or the Press since there is an unwritten law which declares it 'bad form' for either pressure groups or the administration to embarrass the other. As Sir Raymond Streat, who for many years looked after cotton interests, remarked, 'You lose the confidence of Whitehall if you try to use Westminster'. [30] M. Joel Barnett argues that it was just this confidence that at least one pressure group in the housing lobby was so anxious to maintain during the passage of the Rent Act (1957) that it played down certain information at its disposal which would have caused political embarrassment. [31]

Many of the contacts at this level are on a personal basis, though advisory committees, both statutory and non-statutory, are inclined to formalise this relationship. At one count the Ministry of Agriculture had fifty-four of these committees. No doubt some of them were looking into obscure subjects, but it would be wrong to think that this was true in every case and to believe that the really big issues of the day were somehow treated differently, in a more open and democratic forum. To illustrate this fallacy both Crick and Hunter referred to the National Economic Development Council or 'Neddy' as it came to be called. [32] Here was a body made up of ministers and pressure group leaders from industry and the trade unions; its purpose was to examine Britain's potential rate and pattern of economic growth. The discussions were taking place behind closed doors, away from parliamentary scrutiny. MPs would receive only the feedback; once more they would be required to identify with the product and not the process itself.

The democratic objection to the decision making process was reinforced by the claim that not only was the process closed it was also inefficient. Only by opening up the dialogue between pressure groups and the administration could this inefficiency be overcome; only then would the right decisions be made and public consent mobilised. The wider significance of this critique was spelt out by

Bernard Crick; 'There is much historical evidence to suggest that in a complex, modern industrial society, decisions which cannot be questioned are likely, in the long run, either to prove obviously inept, or to need violent enforcement that civilised communities should not stomach.'[33] The stakes were high and the Fulton Report on the machinery of central government was later to accept this, arguing that the policy process had to be more open in a bid to improve both 'the quality of ultimate decisions and increase the general understanding of their purpose.'[34] Fulton's recommendations were welcome, they seemed to reinforce a general suspicion that the existing, closed process was somehow inclined towards conservatism, emphasising a tendency to operate from fixed and sometimes unproven assumptions. The dialogue between civil servants and pressure group leaders was altogether too easy, too hostile to anything but incremental change. As John Mackintosh put it:

> All the present disputants have their views and their interests, and they are aware of each other's positions. It is much easier, rather than turn to fundamentals, to resume where the last discussion left off, to accept existing policy and to see whether anyone has shifted or the external facts have altered enough to make marginal adjustments. This is the pattern which makes it so hard to alter established policy in Whitehall . . . [35]

It was just this type of relationship between the Ministry of Agriculture and the National Farmers' Union which led to what Self and Storing clearly regarded as a serious criticism of our agricultural policy makers: their apparent inability to consider alternative methods of agricultural support even when existing methods ran counter to Britain's wider political objectives.[36]

In the mid 1970s it may seem naive to think that Britain's decline had a lot to do with the closed relationship between pressure groups and the administration. Even more naive perhaps was the belief that this decline could be halted by simply tinkering with existing institutions. However, the debate is still of interest for at least two other reasons. In the first place it reinforces the obvious truth that the emerging emphasis on the idea of politics as a play-off between conflicting group interests was not taken up in Britain in a totally self-congratulatory manner. The plight of the unorganised may have received little attention, but at least the idea of government as arbiter of the public interest designed to protect weak groups against strong groups was acknowledged; and there was also the growing conviction that the anonymous relationship between all groups and the administration required, in S.E. Finer's language, more light. To this extent at least the British spirit of enquiry was genuinely critical and to suggest otherwise would be wholly inaccurate. Second, the concern over anonymity and, in particular, the ineffectual role of Parliament, reveals all too clearly the traditional primacy of the Executive in the legislative process. In Britain the Executive has traditionally decided what Bills are to come before Parliament and when they are to be presented. It has controlled the timetable of a Bill's passage through Parliament and, by virtue of its majority in the House of Commons and the norms of party discipline, it has normally been able to guarantee that the Bill will pass unamended by backbench pressure. The present Labour Government's minority position should not obscure the fact that most standard works on the pressure group universe were written when the Executive authority over Parliament was all but complete. Inevitably this has meant that little attention was given to Parliament: if pressure groups could not get what they wanted in their routine contacts with Whitehall then they may as well give up, or that at least was the theory. To be sure, this is perhaps over-stating the case a little. Backbench pressure can and has resulted in changes in government policy and this is particularly likely when a minister finds himself caught between his own backbenchers and the opposition. A good example of this was the Resale Prices Bill, introduced into Parliament early in 1974 by Edward Heath, then President of the Board of Trade and Secretary of State for Industry, Trade and Regional Development. The practice of collective resale price maintenance had been around for a long time and as early as 1949 the Lloyd Jacobs Committee had recommended its abolition. The Cohen Commission (1956) also had its doubts about RPM and by 1963, after two highly revealing reports from the Monopolies Commission, Edward Heath's proposal to limit the practice, as embodied in the Resale Prices Bill, seemed a logical step. There was opposition though, particularly from Conservative backbenchers who made it clear that the Bill was unpopular with many traders and shopkeepers, traditional Tory voters whose loyalty was soon to be put to the test. A well organised Parliamentary campaign against the Bill quickly got underway and the strong possibility that Labour would join the Tory rebels and vote against the government forced the Leader of the House, Selwyn Lloyd, into setting up a steering committee to mediate between Heath and his critics. This tactic worked and the Bill eventually got through, but in the process the evidence reveals that Heath was forced to give way on several points of importance.[37] Backbench pressure was also significant in affecting the content of the Race Relations Act (1965).

As originally drafted racial discrimination in a public place was a criminal offence. This provision was condemned by the Conservative Party in Parliament, who came to rely on the support of a small group of Labour members who argued that criminal sanctions should be replaced by machinery for conciliation. After a defiant stand by the Home Office, conciliation won the day. Parliamentary arithmetic had forced the government's hand. [38]

In the case of resale price maintenance, and in the struggle for conciliation, pressure groups played their part, the conditions for a Parliamentary initiative were right. More typically though, pressure groups know well enough that if they have failed to persuade the administration they are unlikely to carry Parliament. It is tempting to believe that while this applies to government legislation very different rules apply to private members' bills; to believe that if a pressure group can find an interested member who has won a chance to legislate it can provide him with a bill whose progress has little or nothing to do with the attitude of the administration. This is a misconception. Private members' bills pass only if the government agrees to allow them to pass. On the subject matter of the bill, whether it is on hallmarking or abortion, the government decides. Whether or not a free vote is allowed is largely irrelevant, since that decision too is the government's prerogative, or at least *vis-a-vis* its own supporters.

Most studies of private members' legislation have a good deal to say about the role of 'promotional groups'. But what exactly are 'promotional groups' and how are they different from other pressure groups? This is one of those questions which is easier to ask than to answer. As early as 1955 W.J.M. Mackenzie, while clearly regarding classification as important, suggested caution. He felt that although there appeared to be a distinction between selfish pressure groups and do-good groups the distinction could not always be maintained. [39] Self and Storing were likewise cautious. Indeed, they appear to have been so perplexed by the problem that they wrote a book about pressure groups without actually making use of a classification at all. [40] S.E. Finer, ever pragmatic, acknowledged the many difficulties but threw caution to the wind and reached the conclusion that, ignoring refinements, there remains a 'basic distinction' between pressure groups whose object is to further some interest, say the National Farmers' Union, and those who are promoting some cause such as the Howard League for Penal Reform. [41] This distinction sounds sensible enough but it did not suit everyone. J.D. Stewart, for example, was later to differentiate between sectional and cause groups while Potter preferred spokesmen and promotional groups. [42]

Of crucial importance is not the small differences that help to divide these various attempts at classification, but rather what they share in common, that is, they are all designed as vertical classifications, to use Robert Benewick's term, and tell us nothing about pressure groups in terms of their differential access.[43] Of course, traditional classifications tell us something, but they do not tell us what we really need to know. To understand this it is only necessary to appreciate that pressure groups are out to influence government policy, that is their business, and the extent to which they can hope to achieve this depends, in part, on their access to government and its various agencies and the degree to which they can carry on a structured dialogue. Thus, the fact that some pressure groups have greater access than others is one of the first things that the student of politics ought to know. Traditional classifications have been designed, consciously or unconsciously, to work against this understanding. To tell the student that there is a distinction to be drawn between the National Farmers' Union and the Howard League for Penal Reform is to tell him very little.

To put this right Benewick has suggested an alternative or additional classification which is specifically designed to show the extent to which pressure groups are plugged into the political process. He characterises the pressure group universe as comprising three worlds:

> The first world . . . includes groups, whether interest or promotional, whose access to the decision makers is continuous, resources impressive, legitimacy established, and whose demands are considered to be mainly routine. Some can, and do, impose commanding constraints but when acting as pressure groups it is in their interests to maintain rather than to disturb the balance of power. The TUC and the CBI are outstanding examples.
>
> For second world groups access is more or less accepted although it is likely to be intermittent. Resources are varied yet limited relative to first world groups. They tend to be issue orientated and engender opposition but the balance of power is only marginally affected. Second world groups accept and further consensus. Examples are to be found among the social reform groups . . . Some of the groups establish sponsor-client relations and more properly belong in the first world while others are successful in mobilising support at the Parliamentary level. Considerable attention has been devoted to these groups which may be less important politically than some of those in the third world.

> The third world . . . is more amorphous. The degree to which these groups are recognised varies widely and access is likely to be sporadic. At the same time the groups tend to be highly active and at different levels of the political system. Many cannot meet the requisites for legitimacy and even when they do they remain suspect . . . . It is not just a matter of issue recognition, poverty for example is not denied, but of establishing its priority and promoting its resolution. Since the ultimate satisfaction of their demands may involve a radical re-structuring of society and the re-ordering of priorities they challenge or threaten the balance of power.[44]

There are difficulties associated with Benewick's classification, and not least in his wish to equate it with patterns of international stratification and the use of phrases like 'the balance of power'. However, leaving this aside , what he proposes makes it much easier for students of politics to appreciate that some groups have more access than others and, even more important, the ideological reasons behind this differential access. To be sure, pressure group theorists like Potter have been quick to identify an 'inner circle' of powerful pressure groups and Finer knew well enough that those groups with a hefty 'clout' would be accorded more access than others. However, it was never really emphasised, sometimes never even mentioned, that some groups were regarded as not being legitimate, that they were effectively defined out of the political system or kept at a safe distance because their demands implied a radical restructuring of the social and political order.

That this myopia, to put it charitably, among pressure group theorists was a prop to pluralism is obvious. The idea of a plural society, a society in which politics is about the play-off between groups for marginal gain, is only possible to the extent that all groups accept the same ideological rules. This is the true nature of political consensus. Where the consensus is challenged, where the ideological rules of the game are not accepted, then the politics of compromise is on its way out, the limits of pluralism have been reached. To virtually ignore pressure groups who make such a challenge, to conduct the study of pressure groups as if all groups, in fact, accept the ideological rules of the game, sustains the bias of pluralism and turns theory into myth.

This is not to deny that many important groups in our society do accept the same ideological rules and so see politics as being about little more than the trade-off between rival pressure groups for marginal gain. To this important extent, at least, there is indeed a consensus; Samuel Beer did not somehow import it. However, whether or not the trade-off between rival groups is carried out on equal terms is another matter. Miliband, for example, denies it, arguing that the pluralist paradigm is accurate enough to the extent that trade-offs occur, but where it borders on myth is its often implicit assumption that the major organised interests in our society, capital and labour compete on equal terms. Miliband goes on to suggest that there is no point in looking to government as a corrective in the trade-off between these groups since the leadership of both political parties in Britain accept the political economy largely as it is, with its in-built bias against labour, and this is a view which is reinforced by the advice they receive once in office. [45]

It is not surprising that conventional studies of the pressure group universe have concentrated on first and second world groups since they are the groups which are really plugged into the political system. To study them rather than third world groups is simply to acknowledge that these groups have well cut channels of influence which are susceptible to analysis and critique. They are not in danger of being defined out, they are very much in, a part of the governing process. This brings its own problems: questions about strategy, for example, how and when to press particular demands; questions about a group's internal structure, its relationship with Whitehall and with other groups in the same lobby, and so on. These questions are obviously of considerable importance to the student of politics and they have received a lot of attention. However, to concentrate too much attention on the problems of first and second world groups is to help to obscure the limits of pluralism even further; it is a failure to consider the very real problems faced by third world groups in their struggle to find a meaningful role within the existing political system. How intense, for example, are the internal ideological tensions that result from such a struggle? How does government respond when confronted by what it sees as hostile groups, and how do those groups cope with that response? Concerns like these need to be contrasted with the concerns of pressure groups in the first and second worlds. The contrast is revealing as the example of the Howard League for Penal Reform and Radical Alternatives to Prison will show. The Howard League is a second world group; it is well established and well respected and by virtue of its close relationship with the Home Office shows characteristics which more properly belong to groups in the first world. Radical Alternatives to Prison is a third world group; it is not well established and its legitimacy is in question. RAP's problems are not the problems of the Howard League.

NOTES

[1] Bernard Crick, *In Defence of Politics,* Penguin, Harmondsworth, 1964, p.18.
[2] *American Political Science Review,* vol.XLIV, March 1950, p.742.
[3] Darryl Baskin, *American Pluralist Democracy: A Critique,* Van Nostrand, New York, 1971, chapter 6.
[4] Bernard Crick, *The American Science of Politics,* Routledge and Kegan Paul, London, 1959, p.118-9.
[5] Robert A. Dahl, *A Preface to Democratic Theory,* University of Chicago Press, Chicago, 1956, p.132.
[6] A.F. Bentley, *The Process of Government,* University of Chicago Press, Chicago, 1908, p.358.
[7] Samuel Beer, *Modern British Politics,* Faber and Faber, London, 1965, chapter 5.
[8] Samuel Beer, *Modern British Politics,* Faber and Faber, London, 1965, p.151.
[9] Samuel Beer, *Modern British Politics,* Faber and Faber, London, 1965, p.318.
[10] See, for example, *American Political Science Review,* vol.L, no.1, March 1956, and *Political Quarterly,* vol.XXVI, no.1, 1955.
[11] *Political Quarterly,* vol.XXVI, no.1, 1955.
[12] S.M. Lipset, *Political Man,* Mercury Books, London, 1963, p.406.
[13] W. Kornhauser, *The Politics of Mass Society,* Routledge and Kegan Paul, London, 1960.
[14] W. Kornhauser, *The Politics of Mass Society,* Routledge and Kegan Paul, London, 1960, p.229.
[15] S. Beer, 'Pressure groups and parties in Britain', *American Political Science Review,* vol.LI, no.1, March 1956.
[16] *Political Quarterly,* vol.29, no.1, 1958, p.1; and W.J.M. Mackenzie 'Pressure groups in British Government', *British Journal of Sociology,* vol.VI, no.2, 1955.
[17] Bernard Crick, *The American Science of Politics,* Routledge and Kegan Paul, London, 1959, p.123.
[18] S.E. Finer, *Anonymous Empire,* Pall Mall Press, London, second edition, 1966, p.121.
[19] S.E. Finer, *Anonymous Empire,* Pall Mall Press, London, second edition, 1966.
[20] H. Eckstein, 'The Politics of the BMA', *Political Quarterly,* vol. XXVI, no.4, 1955.
[21] W.J.M. Mackenzie, 'Pressure groups in British Government', *British Journal of Sociology,* vol.VI, no.2, 1955.
[22] S.E. Finer, *Anonymous Empire,* Pall Mall Press, London, second

edition, 1966, p.124.
[23] David B. Truman, *The Governmental Process,* Alfred A. Knopf, New York, 1951, p.511.
[24] S. Beer, 'The British legislature and the problems of mobilising consent', in Bernard Crick (ed.) *Essays on Reform,* Oxford University Press, London, 1967, p.91.
[25] Crick's thesis is outlined in *The Reform of Parliament,* Weidenfeld and Nicolson, London, 1964.
[26] S.A. Walkland, *The Legislative Process in Great Britain,* George Allen and Unwin, London, 1968, p.16.
[27] *British Farmer* (NFU), 8 March 1969, p.40.
[28] J.P. Mackintosh, 'The problems of agricultural politics', *Journal of Agricultural Economics,* vol.21, part 1, 1970.
[29] S.E. Finer, *Anonymous Empire,* Pall Mall Press, London, second edition, 1966, p.22.
[30] Quoted by N. HUnter in 'Power and Parliament, *The Listener,* 25 July 1963.
[31] M. Joel Barnett, *The Politics of Legislation,* Weidenfeld and Nicolson, London, 1969, pp.131–6.
[32] N. Hunter, 'Power and Parliament', *The Listener,* 25 July 1963. For Crick see *The Reform of Parliament,* Weidenfeld and Nicolson, London, second edition, pp.240–41.
[33] Bernard Crick, *The REform of Parliament,* Weidenfeld and Nicolson, London, 1967, p.2.
[34] *The Civil Service,* vol.1 (Report), para.277, HMSO, Cmnd.3638, 1970.
[35] J.P. Mackintosh, 'The problems of agricultural politics', *Journal of Agricultural Economics,* vol.21, part 1, 1970.
[36] P. Self and H. Storing, *The State and The Farmer,* Allen and Unwin, London, 1962, pp.229–30.
[37] S.S. Walkland, *The Legislative Process in Great Britain,* George Allen and Unwin, London, 1968, pp.81–2.
[38] S.E. Finer, *Anonymous Empire,* Pall Mall Press, London, second edition, 1966, pp.76–7.
[39] W.J.M. Mackenzie, 'Pressure groups in British Government', *British Journal of Sociology,* vol.VI, no.2, 1955.
[40] P. Self and H. Storing, *The State and The Farmer,* Allen and Unwin, London, 1962, chapter 1.
[41] S.E. Finer, *Anonymous Empire,* Pall Mall Press, London, second edition, 1966, p.4.
[42] J.D. Stewart, *British Pressure Groups: their role in relation to the House of Commons,* Oxford University Press, London, 1958, p.25. A. Potter, *Organised Groups in British National Politics,* Faber and

Faber, London, 1961, part 1.
[43] Robert Benewick, 'Politics without ideology: the perimeters of pluralism' in R. Benewick, R.N. Berki and B. Parekh (eds), *Knowledge and Belief in Politics,* Allen and Unwin, London, 1973.
[44] Robert Benewick, 'Politics without ideology: the perimeters of pluralism' in R. Benewick, R.N. Berki and B. Parekh (eds), *Knowledge and Belief in Politics,* Allen and Unwin, London, 1973.
[45] R. Miliband, *The State in Capitalist Society,* Weidenfeld and Nicolson, London, 1969.

3 The Howard Association and the Howard League: a synoptic appreciation 1866–1976

Although progressive opinion welcomed the formation of The Howard Association in 1866, it was clear that the Association faced considerable obstacles in its campaign to change official attitudes on matters of penal practice. Not least in this context was the simple tactical problem created by the effective autonomy of most prisons which were administered by local justices of the peace. Therefore, it was not until 1877 when the ownership and control of local prisons was passed to a Board of Commissioners that the Association could begin directing its energies with any real conviction towards the Board, and the Home Office itself, in an attempt to achieve effective national reforms. [1]

But what were these reforms, on what issues did the Association under its secretary, William Tallack, choose to campaign in the last quarter of the nineteenth century? Was its prime concern with the prison system, as perhaps already implied, or was penal reform taken to embrace far wider issues? In the main, the answer is that the Association restricted its attention to the prison system. This is not to say that it never commented on wider issues. Indeed, it was at various stages closely associated with the Society for the Abolition of Capital Punishment and early in the 1880s came out in favour of probation. However, as Gordon Rose has authoritatively commented:

> It was clear that the main interests of the Association were to be in the sphere of prison reform . . . The application of the reformatory idea to adults – classification, productive work, progressive grades and the intermediate prison, and adequate supervision on discharge – these were the core of the Association's policy. [2]

This emphasis on the prison system, and to a lesser extent the welfare of discharged prisoners, are important themes in the Association's history to which we shall frequently return. Suffice it to say at present, that in the years immediately following its foundation the Association's policies on the prison system were in many respects in tune with international reform opinion, with the important exception of Tallack's emphasis on the principle of separation.[3] Possibly as a result of an earlier visit to the Eastern Penitentiary at Philadelphia in the United States Tallack believed passionately in the almost total separation of prisoners by day and night to avoid 'contamination'. In this vein he was vehement in his condemnation of associated labour long after it had been accepted by most other parties in the penal lobby.

The Association contributed to the public debate on penal policy throughout the 1870s. Through its own publications, its evidence to the Royal Commission on Penal Servitude (1879) and many press reports of its activities the Association attracted a growing membership and an annual income at its highest of over £800. All this contributed considerably to the Association's prestige *vis-a-vis* the bureaucracy. True, the Prison Commission's first chairman Sir Edward du Cane did not welcome what was considered as outside interference, but he was eventually forced to reach a form of working compromise with Tallack and by 1886 the Association's Annual Report was pleased to comment that: 'The Committee of the Howard Association have to acknowledge the courtesy which they have experienced from the authorities, and especially from Colonel Sir E.F. du Cane, KCB, during the past year.'[4] To some extent this appears to have been an accommodation of convenience since both Tallack and du Cane came together in an alliance against what they felt to be over-liberal suggestions for penal reform which were then gaining ground in America. By the 1880s, then, the views of the Howard Association and the Prison Board were, in important respects, coming together.[5] This developing symbiosis, however, was publicly called into question by the events leading up to the appointment of the Gladstone Committee in 1894.

The penal system had not been without its critics in the early 1890s. Irish Nationalists in the House of Commons who had been imprisoned for brief periods were not impressed by their treatment, and used Parliamentary time to spell out the degrading consequences of prison routines. But more important, W.D. Morrison, who was closely associated with the Humanitarian League, published a series of highly polemical articles in the *Daily Chronicle* which castigated the British penal system as being essentially pitiless and obsolete. To put matters right Morrison also made specific proposals for reform. These articles aroused much interest which, as Gordon Rose spells out, shows just how decisively the Howard Association had been outflanked by more radical and outspoken reformers:

These articles, strongly supported by the leader column, brought a flood of letters, most of them supporting the proposals. Amongst these, there was one from an ex-prison officer who asked: 'What has the Howard Society been doing all these years?' This brought a long reply from Tallack, who maintained, correctly, that many of the criticisms in the articles had been made by the Association on numerous occasions. There was, however, an unbridgeable gap between Tallack, on the one hand, and the *Daily Chronicle*, the Humanitarian League and W.D. Morrison, on the other. For what the new school of reformers wanted was not so much detailed reforms, upon many of which there was agreement, but a complete change in the balance between deterrence and reformation. They were much less concerned than Tallack with the need to preserve severity of treatment as a measure of prevention, and much more insistent that constructive measures should be brought to bear. They saw separation as an unnecessary hardship, purely negative in its operation, and operating as a bar to the introduction of rehabilitation measures which could only economically be carried out in association. [6]

And what is more to the point, the Gladstone Committee supported this brand of radical reform and came out strongly in favour of more association for purposes of work; it also made a whole range of other important recommendations aimed at liberalising the penal system. Tallack, who had given evidence to the Committee on the dangers of association, was unimpressed, and the Howard Association went so far as to suggest that the Committee had been unduly influenced by some crude arguments unsupported by reliable facts. Such accusations led to a blunt rejoinder from the Humanitarian League:

At the present critical moment, when a great measure of humane reform has been recommended by the Departmental Committee on Prisons, and could certainly be obtained from the new authorities if demanded by all sections of humanitarians, we are all compelled to ask, 'Where is the Howard Association . . . ' It cannot be denied that there is a deep conviction among those who are working most strenuously for the humanising of our prisons, that the Howard Association is no longer a progressive, but a reactionary institution. [7]

There was little Tallack could do to salvage his reputation before he retired in 1901. His penal philosophy was generally too punitive, and although his emphasis on separation seems to imply important assumptions about the criminal's potential for rational choice and action, he had joined du Cane and the Prison Board in advocating a tough prison regime which, as the nineteenth century drew to a close, did little to enhance the status of the Howard Association as a progressive force in the penal lobby.[8]

After Tallack's departure the Association operated in a low key until the outbreak of war in 1914. It is doubtful if its policies had any significant influence on official thinking during the prewar period and its lack of success can perhaps be gauged by the emergence of the Penal Reform League in 1907 which came into being as a direct consequence of the experiences of the Suffragettes. The Suffragettes were the first middle class people to suffer imprisonment in any numbers.[9] Further, their tough treatment in Holloway very quickly came to symbolise all that was worst in British penal practice. The radical conscience was prodded into action and the effectiveness of the existing penal lobby publicly challenged by the very formation of the League under the guidance of Arthur St. John. Although it may well be true that the issues which interested the Suffragettes most, such as forcible feeding and whether or not they were political prisoners, came to occupy only a small fraction of the League's efforts as time went by, it is also clear that the League continued to raise these points.[10] The Howard Association, on the other hand, hardly mentioned them at all.[11] Such caution no doubt stemmed from the Association's genuine disapproval of Suffragette tactics, but equally relevant must have been the Association's wish, even in the face of such penal barbarity, to retain its friendly links with the Prison Commissioners who were under public attack for their treatment of the unfortunate Suffragettes.

Suffragette agitation ended with the start of the war when the penal lobby switched its attention to the plight of conscientious objectors. In a way, of course, many of the conscientious objectors were quite capable of looking after themselves. As middle class intellectuals they were able to articulate their distaste for the barbarities of the prison system, and none more so than Stephen Hobhouse who wrote the influential *An English Prison from Within.* Hobhouse not only went onto join the Penal Reform League, but more important, his family connections with the Webbs led directly to the setting up of the Prison System Enquiry under the guidance of the Labour Research Department in the Labour Party.[12] The Webbs themselves served on this Committee which also included Margery Fry, by this time secretary of the Penal Reform League.

At about this time Margery Fry engineered an amalgamation

between the Penal Reform League and the Howard Association. It is probably true that the amalgamation benefitted both groups in that both were small enough to benefit from almost any attempt to enlarge their active support, but it is difficult to escape the conclusion that the Howard Association, finance apart, got the best of the bargain. The Penal Reform League was more active, appealed more readily to critical, reforming intellectuals like the Hobhouses, Fenner Brockway and Dorothy Scott, and in the person of Margery Fry the Howard Association placed its future in the hands of one of the most able and socially well connected reformers of the inter-war period. [13] In fact, it was Margery Fry who took over the detailed running of the newly created Howard League, leaving Cecil Leeson, the League's official full time secretary to concentrate his efforts on the embryonic Magistrates' Association. [14]

The publication of the Report of the Prison System Enquiry Committee in 1922 is widely regarded as a landmark in the campaign for penal reform. The direct influence of the Report though is not altogether easy to define, since, as has been pointed out elsewhere, the new Prison Commissioners were already committed to a more liberal regime. [15] The broad arrow was discontinued; the silence rule less rigidly adhered to, educational provision increased, and so on. True, the budget deficit which followed the collapse of the short post war boom led to Treasury cuts across almost the entire spectrum of the social welfare services, including the prison system. But even this it seems did not dampen the enthusiasm of the Howard League which, until the mid 1920s at least, felt reasonably hopeful about the gathering strength of penal reform. To what extent this optimism was justified is doubtful. Prison life continued to be barbarous, a point which was soon to be reinforced by the riot at Dartmoor prison in January 1932. This brutal episode in which two prisoners were shot and many others injured during a police baton charge was the subject of an immediate government enquiry which served as a blunt reminder to all the parties concerned that there was much still to be accomplished before the prison system was to reach its humane, correctional ideal.

This is not to suggest that there were no gains. On the contrary, the first open prison came into operation near Wakefield, and although these prisons now seem to have an uncertain future, the opening of New Hall Camp in 1936 was seen as a great step forward. Very different, but equally significant in its own way, was the regular payment of convicted prisoners for work done, a notable reform given that it was achieved during the years of economic depression. The Howard League, and particularly Champion Russell, had an important role to play in this reform, raising money to pay special class prisoners in Wakefield prison for their work during a trial period starting in October 1929. The scheme was soon extended and Gordon Rose has claimed that: 'The initiation of this important reform was undoubtedly directly due to the League.'[16]

The League did not concentrate exclusively on the prison system. Indeed, one of its most spectacular successes came through its achievement of legal aid for the poor, when in 1927 it drafted a Private Member's Bill which proposed making legal aid much more easily available in courts of summary jurisdiction and also in higher courts. The Home Office was consulted to sort out any difficulties, the League's Parliamentary group mobilised and eventually R.H. Turton piloted through the House a measure which became the Poor Prisoners' Defence Act (1930). This very considerable success for the League was added to by the Summary Jurisdiction (Appeals) Act of 1933 which extended legal aid to appeals. This measure was passed through Parliament with the help of Sir John Withers and R.H. Turton who again did well in the Private Members ballot.[17] Not surprisingly the League values these achievements and even today they are used to bolster its status in the penal lobby.

Compared with this success over legal aid it was to the League's considerable regret that it had nothing like the same impact on government policies towards the young offender. It contributed evidence to the influential Departmental Committee on Young Offenders which was appointed in 1925 and found much to support in that Committee's final and wide ranging recommendations, especially its concern to provide observation centres where young offenders could be sent, 'reported upon and tested.'[18] The psychologist like the psychiatrist was coming strongly to the fore in the League's armoury for the assessment and treatment of offenders of all ages, and the League's association with the Institute for the Study and Treatment of Delinquency (ISTD) founded later in the 1930s is not surprising.[19] In the meantime, the League faced with some bitterness the translation of the Departmental Committee's recommendations into a Bill in December 1931 which deliberately excluded observation centres on the grounds of economy. Combine this with a Lords' inspired amendment to facilitate birching, which was comfortably passed in the Commons, and it is no wonder that on the question of young offenders the League felt so plainly disappointed.

On the general question of corporal punishment, though, official opinion moved strongly towards abolition in the years that followed. A memorial on the subject from the Howard League in 1935 helped to sustain the pressure for reform and two years later a Departmental Committee on Corporal Punishment was established under the chairmanship of Edward Cadogan. It was mainly thanks to the work of this Committee and the evidence it received from the Home Office that a clause to abolish corporal punishment outside prisons appeared in the Criminal Justice Bill (1938). This evidence demonstrated beyond much doubt that the deterrent effects of flogging and birching were nothing like as great as the retentionists had always claimed and the government were convinced that abolition was the only course it could reasonably follow. Such a conclusion was particularly gratifying to the League's chairman, George Benson, who had campaigned vigorously against corporal punishment and in collaboration with the psychiatrist Edward Glover (a founder member of the ISTD) had written a pamphlet on the subject in the early thirties.

The Howard League was active on a number of other fronts in the 1930s, from the campaign to abolish capital punishment to its very real and growing concern over the efficiency of the Discharged Prisoners Aid Societies. However, by 1938 the League was much more preoccupied by the impending Criminal Justice Bill, a measure of great importance, but none the less one which eventually had to be deferred until after the war. In any detail, then, this Bill waits for our attention at a later stage but the prewar preparations leading up to the Bill are immediately relevant since they indicate just how far the League had progressed since the amalgamation in 1921. For example, no sooner had Sir Samuel Hoare at the Home Office made it clear through the King's Speech that legislation was intended than a memorandum suggesting reforms on behalf of the League was circulated in Parliament drawing support from almost 200 MPs.[20] This was accomplished through the Parliamentary Penal Reform Group which had been set up by the League in March 1924 and between the wars was a constant source of pressure on successive governments. But, and as any close student of the British political process will emphasise, Parliamentary pressure is no real substitute for close and persuasive contacts with the bureaucracy. In this context the League was also in a strong position since, from its very early days under the sure hand of Margery Fry, it had moulded close personal and official relationships with senior government officials.[21] So much so that Sir Alexander Paterson from the Prison Commission, who had served with Margery Fry on the Prison System Enquiry Committee and earlier befriended Stephen Hobhouse, and Sir Alexander Maxwell from the Home Office felt it quite in order to attend a Howard League Executive Committee meeting to explain the government's thinking on certain sections of the Criminal Justice Bill (1938).[22] This easy interchange between ruling elites, so much a feature of the British political system during this period, is perhaps best symbolised in the person of Sir Samuel Hoare who introduced the Criminal Justice Bill in 1938 as Home Secretary and then spoke in the House of Lords on its reintroduction in 1947 as Lord Templewood, President of the Howard League.

To what extent the League's close identification with, and access to, the bureaucracy during the inter-war years was possibly harmful is certainly a legitimate matter for assessment and critique. It may well be that so close an association then, or later, placed constraints on the League's independent action. Gordon Rose, however, gives no hint at all that the League was in any sense subject to bureaucratic colonisation during the inter-war period at least, and even if this judgement is treated with considerable caution, there is little doubt that the League was an advance on its reactionary predecessor, the Howard Association. Indeed, with its advocacy of a progressively more liberal prison system and the classification and treatment of convicted criminals by the more 'scientific' methods being developed in psychology and psychiatry the League seemed a powerful and benevolent force in the prewar penal lobby.

In the years immediately preceding the war the penal lobby had an air of optimism, which was by no means unjustified. In 1938 the total number of indictable offences was less than 300,000, while the daily average prison population of England and Wales was proportionately one of the lowest prison populations in the world. These encouraging figures were shattered by the war. The daily average prison population rose sharply and between 1939 and 1945 the number of indictable offences, and of persons convicted of them, increased by 50 per cent.[23] Faced with what appeared to be a steadily increasing crime wave the government reintroduced a revised Criminal Justice Bill in 1947 which was much more punitive than its predecessor. The Howard League was far from happy with the revised Bill. In particular, it opposed the introduction of residential detention centres in place of attendance centres, the omission of state remand homes and the proposal to extend the maximum period of preventive detention from 10 to 14 years. It was also a matter of regret to the League that, whereas the Criminal Justice Bill (1938) had placed a complete bar on imprisoning young offenders under sixteen, the revised Bill put this at seventeen for courts of summary jurisdiction and fifteen for higher courts. Although unimpressed by other aspects of the Bill it was largely, though by no means exclusively, on these issues that the League concentrated its efforts.[24]

In many ways the lobby to amend the Criminal Justice Bill (1947) is a classic example of the Howard League's ability to get the best out of an unsympathetic Executive. The precise details are not perhaps significant but both revealing and impressive is the extraordinary thoroughness with which the Howard League's Executive Committee prepared its ground, combing through the new Bill clause by clause, drawing up tightly worded amendments and then communicating these amendments through carefully timed meetings to their supporters on the relevant Parliamentary committees. This was only a beginning since the Bill thus amended had to be considered and tactics decided for its passage through the Lords. The League's industry was not unrewarded. Lord Templewood succeeded with an amendment to make attendance centres possible in a modified form, the limit to the restitution that an offender could be ordered to pay as a condition of probation was raised from £25 to £100 and, as a result of another amendment, any time spent in custody pending appeal beyond six weeks was to count as part of the sentence. Altogether the League claimed credit for ten changes to the Bill.[25] Not all of these changes were highly significant, and it must be admitted that on several important issues the government simply ignored the League's opinion and pressed on regardless. The government refused, for example, to retain probation without conviction and also stuck to its tougher line on allowing more young offenders to face the possibility of imprisonment.

To a large extent the government's attitude was a direct response to growing public concern over the rising crime rate and the widespread demand – frequently supported in Parliament at this time – for tougher penalties which, it was felt, were needed to halt this trend. In such a punitive climate, and with the government so firmly committed to the main lines of its Bill, the League could only have hoped for the modest Parliamentary success which it eventually achieved. Further concessions might have been won by adopting more aggressive tactics, but this the League decided was not its style. During the inter-war years it had worked hard to achieve the confidence and respect of the bureaucracy and it was not prepared to upset its pattern of friendly and informal contacts by precipitating a public row. This low profile left the League open to the charge that it was not doing enough, that it was starting to drift like its predecessor the Howard Association into the arms of the bureaucracy. The Prison Medical Reform Council (PMRC) clearly took this view. Formed in 1943, the Council had the support of many conscientious objectors who were only too willing to heap abuse on the Prison Board, and, *inter alia,* to question the achievements of the Howard League. This led to a frankly unprecedented 'scene' at the League's AGM in 1945 when two members of the PMRC got themselves elected onto the Executive Committee. This election did nothing to alter the League's style. Indeed, it only served to reinforce the Executive Committee's view that the PMRC was an irresponsible and noisy organisation given to the publication of inaccurate and damaging statements. The suggestion that the two organisations should amalgamate, so enabling the League to benefit from an injection of new, young and enthusiastic members was firmly turned down by the Executive Committee.[26] The League's chairman George Benson was clearly appalled by the suggestion. This was not surprising since Benson in particular had very easy access to the Home Office and he was not prepared to jeopardise this for the support of what he thought of as a bunch of ill informed rowdies. What Benson had to lose should not be underestimated, and since the origin of his First Offenders Act (1958) can be traced back to the years following the war it is worth looking at it in some detail to illustrate just why the Howard League was so anxious to keep the PMRC at a very safe distance.

The Criminal Justice Act (1948) laid down that before a court could send an adolescent to prison it must first examine and consider all alternative methods of treatment. This did not mean that prison was ruled out in any sense, only that other methods of treatment should be considered first and reasons given if they were thought to be inappropriate. The impact of the new provision was dramatic. Almost immediately the number of adolescents sent to prison dropped by half. Magistrates had been put on the spot and their uncritical use of the prison sentence crudely exposed. George Benson was so impressed by the success of the new provision that he sought to extend it to adult first offenders and this possibility was then considered in depth by a subcommittee of the Home Office Advisory Council on the Treatment of Offenders (ACTO). George Benson and Margery Fry were both appointed to this subcommittee, the outcome of which was the First Offenders Bill, drawn up by the Home Office and presented to Parliament under the Ten Minute Rule by George Benson in February 1958.[27]

With the government's firm support the Bill had an easy passage through the Commons. No divisions were called and the principal argument against the measure, namely, that imprisoning adult first offenders had always shown a high success rate (so why change?) was countered by Benson who argued that: 'The astonishing thing is that all types of sentence give exactly the same result in the case of first offenders – the success rate is always not less than 80 per cent.'[28] The argument then became: why bother to imprison adult first offenders, with its known disadvantages, when other sentences will achieve comparable results? Benson drew on several academic authorities to substantiate this, starting with the Gluecks.

With an undivided House of Commons the Bill's passage in the Lords was obviously secure. The Howard League's President, Lord Templewood, introduced the Bill and Lord Chorley, a distinguished Vice President, summed up the whole cosy Parliamentary achievement in the following Lordly language:

> I think that the Howard League for Penal Reform, with which the noble Viscount [Templewood] has been associated for a long time as its President, can claim a certain amount of kudos in respect of this Bill, in that the Bill was piloted through another place by the Chairman of the League's Executive Committee; and in your Lordships' House is going, I hope, to have an equally smooth passage under the pilotage of the noble Viscount. As one of the noble Viscount's Vice Presidents, it gives me particular personal pleasure to support him . . . .'[29]

Although it is obviously difficult to believe that people actually talk like Lord Chorley, the message is plain enough; the Howard League had the inside track and it was not in business to join the Prison Medical Reform Council in throwing bricks at the political establishment or, more to the point, upsetting the civil service which had become so receptive over the years to the League's unobtrusive pressure.

The same considerations were later to have an important part to play in determining the Howard League's position in the lobby against capital punishment. Between the wars the main pressure for abolition had come from Roy Calvert and the National Council for the Abolition of the Death Penalty. Although the National Council had some success in getting its message across, most notably through the publication of Roy Calvert's *Capital Punishment in the 20th Century*, public opinion remained firmly opposed to abolition and the proceedings of the Select Committee on Capital Punishment in 1929 showed clearly enough that Parliament too had serious doubts. The League's role during this period was tangential, but by no means insignificant. Roy Calvert, for example, used the League's resources to collect information for his book and the National Council knew well enough that it could usually rely on the League's public support.

Towards the end of the war the National Council moved into the Howard League's premises. This temporary arrangement turned out to have very real advantages in the immediate post war years as both organisations set out to persuade the newly elected Labour Government to include an abolition of the death penalty clause in the proposed Criminal Justice Bill. This task of persuasion was no easy matter. The Howard League was quickly off the mark, enlisting the support of nearly 200 MPs, but this seems to have had very little immediate impact on the Home Secretary, Chuter Ede. A deputation from the National Council turned out to be equally unsuccessful. Indeed, members of the deputation came to the sorry conclusion that they had made 'a mistake in assuming that the Home Secretary and his advisors were cognizant of the elementary facts of the case'.[30] There were, of course, limits to the extent of Chuter Ede's authority, that is, he might not wish to include an abolition clause, but there was little he could do to stop an amendment to that effect. It was precisely this knowledge, and the growing evidence of backbench unrest over the government's reticence, that finally forced Chuter Ede to capitulate and allow Sydney Silverman's abolition amendment to be the subject of a free vote at the Report stage. The result was a dramatic victory for the abolitionists. This triumph, however, was short-lived as the House of Lords lost no time in overthrowing the new clause and with this defeat the controversy over the death penalty subsided. In October 1948 the National Council voted to carry on its future activities under the auspices of the Howard League. Members of the National Council were asked to transfer their subscriptions to the League on the understanding that a separate committee on the death penalty would be formed.[31] It was this committee which later prepared the League's evidence to the Royal Commission on Capital Punishment which was appointed late in 1949.

The death penalty issue was kept in the public eye by several sensational murder trials. Timothy Evans, Derek Bentley and Christie were all hanged during the time the Royal Commission was sifting evidence and preparing to report. Pressure for another attempt to legislate on abolition was building up, and this was duly made in a Commons debate on the Report from the Royal Commission. The abolitionists were again defeated, and a few months later in August 1955 the National Campaign for the Abolition of Capital Punishment was founded under the leadership of Victor Gollancz, Arthur Koestler and Canon Collins.

The Howard League was approached by Gollancz in the expectation that its secretary would serve in an official capacity on the National Campaign's Executive Committee.[32] The League was wary of this offer for several reasons. First, it was a multi-purpose organisation and it did not want to be linked too formally with the single issue of capital punishment. Second, the National Campaign intended to hold mass rallies and distribute propaganda on a large scale; from a financial point of view the League could not afford to be associated with such a commitment. Third, and this was almost certainly the decisive factor, the Howard League, as might be surmised, was not disposed to mass campaigns, the pressure of public agitation. As the Executive Committee phrased it:

> The Howard League was an old-established association, basing its case for abolition on factual information collected by Roy Calvert and others, and its reputation for a balanced presentation of the case was important. It could, however, unofficially assist the Campaign, which would probably run for about two years. [33]

The Howard League's apparent monopoly of 'balance' may seem presumptuous. On the other hand, the Executive Committee was right in anticipating that the National Campaign would conduct a fairly vigorous propaganda war causing offence to some of the League's official contacts.

Against this it might be argued that the League needed a more forceful ally, and that however ineptly the National Campaign may have acted on occasions, it did at least revitalise the lobby against the death penalty and force a reluctant Conservative Government to pass its own Homicide Act (1957), which introduced the distinction between capital and non-capital murders, all within the space of two years. There is much to support this interpretation, though it should not be taken as a harsh reflection on the Howard League whose contribution, though less vigorous, was arguably as decisive. The particular and constructive side of the relationship between the National Council and the Howard League has been shrewdly summarised by Christoph:

> Because they shared a common purpose, the two types of groups were able to supplement rather than compete with each other, so that in practice they were able to divide the labour, the Howard League providing much of the research, contacts with government and the world of criminology, and a reputation for integrity and the . . . Campaign the larger membership, finances and propaganda. The particular symbiosis was made necessary by the fact that the Howard League was not equipped for or desirous of engaging in a large scale campaign for abolition, especially since it felt that to do so would jeopardise its standing with the Home Office and prison officials and rebound against its

other penal reform activities.[34]

With the passing of the Homicide Act (1957) the abolitionists paused for breath. It was not long, however, before it became clear that the new Act gave rise to serious anomalies. The distinction between different categories of murder turned out to be very difficult to apply in practice, at least with any sense of justice. Matters came to a head and in 1960 the National Campaign for the Abolition of the Death Penalty was revived under the joint leadership of Victor Gollancz and Gerald Gardiner. The widespread public disquiet over the operation of the Act was reflected in April of the following year when thousands of people filled the Albert Hall and a collection in support of the Campaign raised over £2,000.[35] As things turned out then, whereas the Homicide Act (1957) had been enacted to propitiate the abolitionists, its actual operation only succeeded in reinforcing their determination to press on with their cause to its logical conclusion.

The abolitionists did not have long to wait for their first advance. Harold Wilson's newly elected Labour Government (1964) gave a firm commitment to allow time for the capital punishment issue to be argued out and by December 1964 Sidney Silverman's Murder (Abolition of the Death Penalty) Bill came up for its second reading. Although the Committee stage saw fierce resistance from the retentionists who used various procedural devices to kill off the Bill, the measure was eventually passed by the Commons and sent to the Lords where, to many observers' surprise, it won a relatively easy majority. What the new Act did in effect was to abolish capital punishment for an experimental period of five years. There was no guarantee that suspension would last beyond the experimental period; much would depend, it was felt, on what happened to the murder rate. The Howard League therefore took on what seemed to be the important task of monitoring those Home Office statistics which would eventually be used as the public yardstick for judging the success of Silverman's Act. The fate of those statistics which appeared in the Home Office Report on Murder (1957–68) was perhaps predictable; they were used by both sides in support of completely opposite arguments. The Howard League went so far as to question the credibility of the whole exercise and this was not an untenable position, given the very real problems of definition.[36] The League's doubts were reinforced by a Home Office refusal to publish the results of a study on the murder statistics being carried out by two of its members at Bedford College because its figures did not tally with those in the Home Office Report. The Howard League could have caused the Home Office considerable embarrassment if it had chosen to seriously challenge this refusal. As it happened, statistics seemed largely irrelevant to the final phase of the debate. Somehow Parliament had got used to living without the death penalty and was reluctant to take the positive step of reintroducing it, even in a limited form. Abolition therefore became permanent at the end of the experimental period and the Howard League was left to claim that: 'Capital punishment has been abolished for ever'.[37]

In the long progress towards abolition the Howard League's emphasis on research might be regarded by some as simply a reflection of its wider contribution to the development of British criminological research. There is a lot of evidence to support this view, but a total picture of that contribution is as yet fragmentary. Before the war, as Leon Radzinowicz has pointed out, there was little in the way of serious criminological research, with the exception of Cyril Burt's controversial study, *The Young Delinquent,* first published in the mid-twenties, and the work of the Institute for the Study and Treatment of Delinquency with its early bias towards psychological medicine.[38] This situation was very far from satisfactory, and in 1936 Margery Fry wrote to Alexander Maxwell at the Home Office arguing for a systematic start on research. To refer to this as a milestone is perhaps misleading, since the approach received only a very modest response.[39] Maxwell approached All Souls' College which later gave Max Grünhut financial support. Even allowing for Max Grünhut's later and eminent contribution to British criminology this whole episode can hardly be regarded as a great leap forward, and certainly it did nothing to pacify the Howard League. Perhaps the least that can be said about Margery Fry's approach is that it helped to concentrate Maxwell's mind on research so that in 1938 he was at least talking positively about the necessity for more information on 'practices and results' and the need to examine 'theories and principles'.[40] At the same time Hermann Mannheim, who was later to dominate academic criminology in this country, was struggling to get a permanent position at the LSE.

Clearly then, the government responded very slowly to the need for research and the situation did not change much in the years immediately following the war. The publication of the Criminal Justice Bill illustrates the point perfectly; it contained no provision for the government itself to undertake research or for its funding elsewhere. It was left to backbench pressure to correct this official myopia at the Report Stage. This improvement to the Bill brought no immediate benefits. No money was allowed for research in the estimates until 1951–52, and even then it only amounted to £1,500. No doubt this money was efficiently used by Mannheim and Leslie

Wilkins in their borstal prediction study, and also by Max Grünhut and Leon Radzinowicz who received smaller amounts, but it was absurdly short of what was really needed. As George Benson of the Howard League was to phrase it: 'In relation to our ignorance £1,500 is a pitiful sum.'[41]

It is possible that without Benson's intervention no money at all would have been voted. Briefly, Benson was developing his interest in the prediction studies of the Gluecks around this time, and this led him to ask for an improvement in the criminal statistics. To look into this possibility the Home Office appointed a Working Party which was advised by Benson, Grünhut, Mannheim and Radzinowicz, plus others, that research was as important as developing the criminal statistics. That the Working Party obviously took this advice to the direct benefit of some of its academic advisors is perhaps obvious enough, but more to the point is the claim of T.S. Lodge that the experience of the Working Party, with its exchange of ideas on research and its close association with the appointment of a Home Office Statistical Advisor, influenced official as well as university research methods for the next twenty years, and more.[42] Lodge chooses to emphasise that it was Benson's complaint which led to the decision to form the Working Party. It would be absurd to infer from this that the statistical and research developments which the Working Party foreshadowed would not have happened if it had not been for the chairman of the Howard League with his liking for statistics, which is what George Benson meant by scientific criminology. Yet it has to be remembered that both Grünhut and Mannheim were also members of the Howard League's Executive Committee at this time, and it is not unreasonable to suggest that through these three figures the League had at least a modest influence on the developing style of Home Office criminology.

Unfortunately for the League its quiet influence on the Working Party was not matched by sufficient political clout to push the Treasury into allowing more funds. Thus, by 1955–56 the annual amount spent on research had risen to a mere £2,500. Good research had been completed, and more projects were being planned, but by no stretch of the imagination were the available resources anything like acceptable. This deficiency was soon recognised by R.A. Butler who was appointed as Home Secretary early in 1957. Mr Butler's overall strategy was contained in the White Paper, *Penal Practice in a Changing Society,* published in February 1959.

The assumption which underpinned the White Paper's approach to research was that delinquency cannot be effectively dealt with without a greater understanding of its causes, and without more accurate means of measuring the success of the various treatment methods used to control it. Research into these areas of difficulty was as important as research in the fields of technology and science. The penal lobby endorsed this as a sound base from which to start, and there were few objections raised to the White Paper's later emphasis on assessing treatment methods rather than investigating causes. A survey of past and current research was included and the government's plans for its future development were outlined as a cooperative venture between the recently formed Home Office Research Unit and outside bodies, including universities.[43] The hoped-for goal was clearly stated:

> If this course is patiently pursued, it is hoped and believed that knowledge of crime and criminals will increase to the point at which measures can be taken to bring about a real reduction in the amount of crime and still more effective treatment can be given to each offender.[44]

This brand of steady optimism appealed to the Howard League, and its secretary welcomed the White Paper in its entirety as a major contribution to the on-going debate on penal policy. Mr Butler had impressed the Howard League's hierarchy from the very beginning. He had the sort of confidence to ask them for suggestions, and even to meet with them unaccompanied by his civil servants. In fact, Mr Butler showed all the signs of being a resourceful political heavyweight.

It was in this receptive atmosphere that the Howard League had first approached the Home Secretary in 1957 with the suggestion for an Institute of Criminology. Given the Home Secretary's early commitment to research as a main priority it was inevitable that the League would attempt to formulate its own proposals about how that commitment should work out in practice. It is clear from the League's minutes during the summer of 1957 that there was a strong feeling against research being narrowly interpreted to mean nothing more than prediction studies. Why not, argued one member, make a useful start by researching into what actually goes on in penal institutions. There was an equally strong reaction to the separate but by no means unrelated possibility that any extra resources might be weighted too heavily in favour of the Home Office at the expense of the universities. Discussion also strayed into the area of teaching. The idea of a certificate and/or diploma geared to members of the Prison Service and the Probation Service was canvassed, and it seems that an approach to the Home Office along these lines had already been made. Finally, in order to coordinate the work of the different faculties, colleges and universities Margery Fry suggested that an Institute of Criminology might be established.

Although the research strategy outlined in *Penal Practice in a Changing Society* differs in certain respects from the emphasis suggested by the Howard League, it is by no means entirely at odds with it, except perhaps for Mr Butler's intention to establish an Institute of Criminology at Cambridge. The idea of an Institute had first been taken up with Mr Butler in a letter he had received from Hugh Klare in June 1957, and a few weeks later the Home Secretary discussed the possibility in more depth with Margery Fry herself and Lord Drogheda, Chairman of the Advisory Council on The Treatment of Offenders. Miss Fry did not intend the Institute to have anything like the autonomy it was later to acquire, and she certainly had no liking for the proposal that it should be centred on the Department of Criminal Science in Cambridge with its close interest in criminal law, and the absence in Cambridge of strong departments of sociology, social psychology and psychiatry.[45] This would militate against the multi-disciplinary tradition of British criminology which the Howard League so strongly favoured. There was probably no-one better equipped to argue the League's case than Margery Fry. Her long membership of the University Grants Committee (1919–48), and her post war service on its influential subcommittee on social sciences, had given her many valuable insights into both the academic and practical difficulties surrounding university organisation and development. She was, then, a knowledgeable pressure group spokesman with her feet very firmly on the ground and her preference for an Institute at London rather than Cambridge must have made Mr Butler hesitate. Finally though, Cambridge was preferred, to the very real disappointment of the Howard League. Hugh Klare was later to comment:

> Cambridge was so terribly staid at the time . . . No psychology, psychiatry, or sociology. Mannheim, the father of British criminology, was at the London School of Economics and there was a terrific constellation of talent at other institutes in London to cross fertilise the new science.[46]

Although perhaps a slight over statement, this reflects well enough the League's original hostility towards the new Cambridge Institute. In private, criticism along these lines was to continue and as late as 1962 an influential member of the League's Executive Committee suggested that there was a need for a second, rival Institute of Criminology to provide more speculative and challenging material than was being offered at Cambridge.[47] Nothing came of this suggestion, and by 1964 the League had modified its opposition to the Cambridge Institute sufficiently to invite its Director, Leon Radzinowicz, to deliver its annual address.

What the Director had to say in his address not only influenced future governments, it also had a very real effect on the Howard League. In a wide ranging paper Radzinowicz traced the development of criminological research in England and came to the generous conclusion that although America was still the foremost laboratory for criminological research, England was second, with other European countries still a little way behind. In short, after a slow and cautious start England was now forging ahead near the very top of the research table. This comforting assessment was soon put into a harsher context by Radzinowicz who proceeded to make a number of trenchant criticisms about the way in which this rapid progress in research was not being effectively used by governments in the formulation of penal policy. His attack was focussed on the recently announced Royal Commission on the Penal System (1964). He felt its terms of reference, to cover the whole penal system, were too wide, its concern with the philosophy of punishment largely unhelpful, and its actual method of operation anachronistic. The last point is worth expanding since it was to reflect directly on the League's role and credibility. Radzinowicz argued that there was no longer any point in the Commissioners listening to the usual list of interested pressure groups and then cross-examining them to tease out assumptions. Much more productive would be a Commission with authority to mobilise and coordinate research in government and other agencies, to commission research on its own behalf and even to set up expert working parties to discover the vital and necessary information which must be available before any advances in penal policy can be made.

With this attitude it is not difficult to guess how Professor Radzinowicz would have reacted to a distinguished member of the Howard League's Executive Committee who commented *vis-a-vis* the Royal Commission that 'a few useful ideas was all that was required' from the League. [48] This was precisely what was not required. Penal policy in the past may well have been formulated on the basis of what Lord Hailsham once referred to as a potpourri of intelligent suggestions. And it is possible that the Howard League contributed more intelligent suggestions than most. Such an approach, however, was no longer tenable. The research deficit which had been bothering the Howard League for so long and which it had helped meet on issues like Capital Punishment was about to be made good and inevitably would take over from the thoughtful but usually untested advice of a few well-intentioned experts meeting once a month.

Argument along these lines preoccupied and disturbed the League during the mid 1960s as it was encouraged to understand that:

> For years experts have been sitting around a table and making recommendations. These views were still only opinions. Nowadays, one had to have research reports with solid facts to go on, showing that something had been established. That was the new method. . . . [There was] no reason why this should not tie in with the objects of the League. It might be more influential than the old method.[49]

With one or two notable exceptions this line of reasoning was eventually accepted by the Howard League's Executive Committee which became firmly committed to the view that any pressure group wishing to have its opinions taken seriously by governments must base them on information arising from its own research and perhaps even from its own teaching. It was according to this new orthodoxy that the League was encouraged to explore the possibility of amalgamating or merging with the ISTD. The advantages to both groups and the rationale behind the suggestion was neatly summed up thus: 'The Howard League has traditionally put forward ideas and suggestions to the government but was in need of solid backing of research findings and clinical information. The ISTD had such information at its disposal but did not always put forward ideas and proposals.'[50] Although this particular proposal did not come to anything, the League did decide to press ahead with a small research and teaching unit of its own. This was unveiled during the League's centenary year (1966) as the Howard Centre for Penology. But as things turned out, within a few years the Centre had ceased to operate, and the League's scheme for making a significant contribution to research and teaching exposed as a more or less complete failure, although this is not to suggest that the Howard Centre did no good work. That the League suffered a crisis of identity in the mid 1960s is hardly surprising. There was a great deal of confusion in the penal lobby generally. Radzinowicz had delivered a body blow which left most of the lobby's participants wondering which way to turn. The government's procrastination over the fate of the Royal Commission on the Penal System did little to help. Originally set up by Sir Alec Douglas-Home under the chairmanship of Lord Amory, and including Professor Radzinowicz, the Commission had a very difficult time right from the start. Sir Frank Soskice, when he was Home Secretary, is said to have discussed the Commission's future with Lord Amory, and early in 1966 talks were again going on in the Home Office, this time with Mr Roy Jenkins. By April 1966 the Prime Minister announced to the House that there had been doubts among the Commissioners about the relevance of their task, three had resigned and two others, in view of the new circumstances, had also resigned on the basis that the Commission could no longer usefully continue. The government shared this view, and the Royal Commission had therefore been dissolved. Its place was taken by a new advisory body, The Advisory Council on the Penal System, which would be asked to report from time to time on those aspects of the treatment of offenders on which advice was urgently required. The commitment to an *ad hoc* approach was clearly a victory for Radzinowicz. Further, to the extent that the new Advisory Council was composed of more academics than its predecessor (ACTO), it looked as though the government was preparing to exchange the intelligent suggestion for some systematic research. Unfortunately such optimism was misplaced. Roger Hood, for example, has clearly demonstrated that the new Advisory Council's recommendation (through one of its subcommittees) of community service for offenders, and there has hardly been a more important recommendation during the last ten years, was based upon a series of untested assumptions rather than any systematic research. Hood attributes this lamentable state of affairs to:

> The method of approach and resources traditionally associated with government advisory bodies which at best can only lead to suggestions for unstructured 'experiments'. Without facilities for research and academic enquiry their conclusions and recommendations will probably remain 'a potpourri of intelligent suggestions'. . . . [51]

In the light of these comments it is difficult not to take an ironic view of the Howard League's search in the mid 1960s for a new image, a more research-orientated authority. The growth of criminological research seems to have had so little impact on the policy making process that the League could well have drifted along very much as before. After all, with its committee rooms of experts and practitioners, it was still master of the intelligent suggestion.

The 1960s was not an easy decade for the League, even leaving aside its panic over research. The Criminal Justice Bill, introduced in 1960, was discussed against the background of an increase in crime, and public anxiety over crimes of violence culminated in a campaign by the Anti-Violence League which included a series of meetings in Mr Butler's constituency of Saffron Walden.[52] At this point the League stepped in to counter some of the AVL's more extreme propaganda. The usual paradox associated with public anxiety over crimes of violence, a demand for the reintroduction of corporal punishment, was duly acted out in Parliament. The Howard League fought strongly on this issue and what it felt to be the forces of reaction were defeated, though not without a struggle. At the Report Stage of the Criminal Justice Bill fifty-seven Conservative members voted against their government and in favour of corporal punishment.

The floggers were so vocal during the passage of the Criminal Justice Bill that attention was almost diverted from some of the Bill's more important provisions, not that the League managed to get many of these provisions exactly as it would have liked. On the contrary, the League achieved very little. Its demand that the maximum length of time that a youth might be committed (on consecutive terms) to a detention centre should be limited to six months instead of nine was rejected, so too was its suggestion that no offender under twenty-one should be committed to any form of institutional training unless the court had first considered a full social and medical report. The government also decided, against the League's advice, to press ahead with its proposal for a detention centre for girls. With public feeling as it was, the League's battering was perhaps inevitable; small gains like an increase in the maximum number of hours that could be attached to an attendance centre order were all that could be expected.

The pessimistic expectation, particularly in respect of the young, was changed fundamentally by the election of a Labour Government in 1964 and the subsequent publication of its White Paper on *The Child, The Family and The Young Offender* (August 1965). The proposals contained in the White Paper provoked a major controversy which was to continue over several years. The Howard League's contribution to the argument is of special interest, particularly if it is considered in the context of its earlier evidence to Viscount Ingleby's Committee on Children and Young Persons which reported in 1960.

Ingleby's brief was to consider the working of the law relating to juvenile courst, in all its aspects, and to report on whether any changes were required in the existing processes of local authorities to 'prevent or forestall the suffering of children through neglect in their own homes.'[53] The Howard League had difficulty in formulating its evidence because of differences with the Fisher Committee, of which Margery Fry was a member. It was she who agreed to draft its report to the Ingleby enquiry[54] and it was on the basis of this draft report that Margery Fry (and Eileen Younghusband) were invited by the Howard League's Executive Committee to discuss their differences in April 1957. It soon became clear that the Fisher Committee was still committed at this stage to a two-tier structure, a Family Committee and a Family Court, with the emphasis very much on the former which was to be strongly supported by social workers drawn from the newly created Family Departments at local government level. Access to the courts would not be denied to parents who wanted it, though this would be to Family Courts, which would replace the existing system of juvenile courts.

These proposals were far too radical for the Howard League. In particular, it was worried that as Family Committees were not to be courts of law the rules of evidence might not apply, so leaving the door open to local gossip. There was also the problem of finding suitable people to serve on the Family Committees.[55] For these reasons the Howard League felt unable to accept the two-tier structure and although its final submission to the Ingleby Committee refers to non-criminal Children's Courts for those under fourteen, the wider, family-orientated social welfare ethic of the Fisher Committee is almost totally lacking.[56] In many ways the League's reaction is not too surprising since the Fisher proposals would have shattered the traditional pre-eminence of the juvenile courts and also challenged the status of the probation service, and given that the League's subcommittee on Ingleby was composed mainly of magistrates, these possibilities were regarded with considerable anxiety.

How far this left the League behind progressive opinion can be gauged by the proposals outlined in *The Child, The Family and The Young Offender.* In this controversial White Paper the government took as one of its first principles the need to remove young people as far as possible from the jurisdiction of the courts and the stigma of criminality. To facilitate this local authorities were to be empowered to appoint Family Councils to deal with each case as far as possible through negotiations with the parents, and only when no agreement could be reached, or if the facts were in dispute, would referral to a Family Council , made up of social workers in the children's service and other suitably experienced people, be made. The procedures to be adopted were informal, though guided by social enquiry reports to ensure that all the necessary information was available if it was felt that some form of action, such as the placing of the child under supervision, was necessary. The last resort, Family Courts, would be composed of justices selected for their ability to deal with young people and would have jurisdiction over the under-sixteens. Offenders between 17 and 21, who were then dealt with by the ordinary courts, would in future be tried by Young Offenders Courts. This very bald summary of the government's intentions was underpinned by the stated preference for a family service 'to improve the structure of the various services connected with support of the family and the prevention of delinquency.' (para 7)

Immediately these proposals were made public the acrimony began. The principal contending factions have been accurately identified by A.E. Bottoms:

> The main opposition came from lawyers, magistrates, and probation officers. The last group is of particular interest, as they shared much of the psychoanalytic ideology of other social workers; but they also had a long tradition of independence of local authorities, and of service to courts, and it was from this standpoint that their critique was made. On the other side of the debate, the main supporters of the proposals were other social workers, particularly members of the child care service, and many of these talked openly of their gaining through the proposals much more professional prestige and recognition for their service which was still less than twenty years old.[57]

It is difficult to see how the Howard League could have been anywhere but on the side of those who opposed the White Paper, although to what extent the League and other opponents of the White Paper can be said to have succeeded in their campaign to resist the government's proposals is a matter of debate. However, from our point of view the controversy is of interest because it shows just how far the League's commitment to change was dominated by the magisterial bias of its membership. In the 1960s struggle between 'justice' and 'welfare' the League was firmly on the side of justice.

The controversy over juvenile courts did not deflect the Howard League's secretary Hugh Klare from his major interest, prisons and the prison service. It is arguable that Klare knew more about prisons than anyone else in the penal lobby. He visited prisons extensively, won the respect of many governors, and went out of his way to try and accommodate the Prison Officers Association and, most important of all, was a frequent caller at the Home Office Prison Department. It was as a critic of the Prison Department in the 1960s that Klare showed his clear understanding of how the machinery of central government worked, and more to the point, what was inefficient about the way it worked. The Howard League had always opposed any attempt by the Home Office to take over the Prison Commission. When it finally happened with the setting up of the Home Office

Prison Department and the Prison Board in the early 1960s, Hugh Klare remained unconvinced that the new arrangement would secure any real benefits. Indeed, it was not long before the League was being informed that many decisions affecting the prison service were now being made, not in the Prison Board or the Prison Department, but in other Home Office departments. Further, more and more decisions were being given to administrative grade civil servants rather than to those people with service experience. Naturally, the League showed sympathy for the argument that the Establishment Department at the Home Office was operating a unified staffing policy to the disadvantage of specialised departments. A separate personnel policy for the Prison Department might therefore be necessary. The League was also interested in the possibility of a separate budgetary policy for the Prison Department away from the claws of the Treasury which sometimes made decisions without any real understanding of departmental priorities and objectives.[58] It is a matter for conjecture how far it was the League's exploration of a quasi-independent Prison Department which finally helped persuade the government to call in a firm of outside management consultants to assist its own organisation and methods team in an overhaul of both the Prison Department and the Prison Board. But it is clear that in keeping the issue very much towards the top of the Howard League's agenda Klare showed how perfectly he was in touch with what was preoccupying the prison service at the very highest level; and when the time came in 1968 he had learned enough management jargon to translate these preoccupations into a coherent and viable set of ideas which at least tempted the government to listen to his case.[59]

As for prisons, Klare's evidence to the Longford Committee in 1964 demonstrated what most of his admirers would regard as one of his characteristic strengths, a balanced concern for both the prisoner and the prison staff. On the staff side Klare could see no need for the ordinary officer to learn military drill. Indeed, he clearly regarded the whole military ethos of the service as not only nonsense but also dangerously irrelevent in that it obscured what the prison officer should really be training for, namely, a closer involvement with prisoners based on an understanding of group dynamics, role theory and communication studies. In short, the prison officer should aim towards at least a semi-professional status as someone qualified to help in the process of rehabilitation; this would prove to be more rewarding and more constructive than the prison officer's traditional role as mere guard or turnkey.

There was little doubt in Klare's mind that without these developments in the training of prison staff, prisons could not become what he felt they should be, institutions of social learning rather than universities of crime.[60] Only with a suitably qualified staff and, equally crucial, a less rigid regime, could prisoners test themselves in different social roles, confront their personal difficulties and prepare to face the outside world. This very considerable vision, which so much characterised the Howard League during Klare's time as its secretary, could not become a reality without a very real improvement in the physical environment in which prison officers and prisoners alike were forced to live and work. With this in mind the Howard League approached the Prison Department in 1963 with a major rebuilding programme. This included, among many other bold proposals, a scheme to pull down, and then rebuild as local prisons, Pentonville, Holloway and Wandsworth. In total, the programme, which also provided for extensive prison rebuilding in the provinces, amounted to thirty-one new institutions at an estimated cost of around £15 million. It is easy to argue that the Howard League's programme was too ambitious. Equally though, successive governments have failed to avoid chronic overcrowding and this has done little for Klare's rehabilitative ideal. However, the failure to develop a more constructive prison regime is as much the consequence of the Mountbatten enquiry as it is of overcrowding.

In 1966 the spy George Blake made a dramatic escape from prison and shortly afterwards the Home Secretary announced that Lord Mountbatten would head an enquiry 'into recent prison escapes, with particular reference to that of George Blake, and to make recommendations for the improvement of prison security'. The outcome of this enquiry was a fourfold classification of prisoners, from category A to category D, according to their security risk and the degree of danger their escape might bring to the public and police. But more drastic, the enquiry was followed by an increase in government expenditure on reorganising prisons to improve their security. Closed circuit television, searchlights, barbed-wire, day and night guard dog patrols, all these measures followed the Mountbatten enquiry.[61]

In its evidence to the Mountbatten enquiry the Howard League supported, in principle, the idea of classification and also argued in favour of maximum security prisons on the basis that small security wings in local prisons did not provide enough space or facilities for the prisoner serving a long sentence. It was only on the basis that it was the best tactic to get a maximum security prison quickly that the League even felt able to give the enquiry's wide terms of reference limited support. That the League came to regret this modest touch of pragmatism is obvious enough. The prison system after the

Mountbatten Report became even more inflexible and rigid than it had been in the past. Emphasis on the sort of reforms that Hugh Klare had advocated was swept aside in the name of security, and there is more than a touch of despair about the joint Statement issued by the Howard League and the National Association for the Care and Resettlement of Offenders in February 1970. This claimed that rehabilitation was now regarded as a luxury which could no longer be afforded and that the new security drive had reduced the prison service, at all levels, to an anxious and hypersensitive state. Stress was also placed on the under-utilisation of open institutions, a particularly galling development since the Mountbatten Report had specifically gone out of its way to argue that its conclusions should in no way be taken as a criticism of 'the trend towards treatment in open conditions'. (para 208)

Although it is probably fair to suggest that the enquiry's wide terms of reference did not necessarily invite the Report's conclusions and the subsequent draconian measures, it is doubtful if the prison system would have suffered such a severe setback if Mountbatten had been confined to the case of George Blake. It is tempting to believe that the terms of reference were really dictated by a number of sensationally reported escapes which occurred at about the same time as Blake's escape from Wormwood Scrubs and that in reacting as he did the Home Secretary was simply responding to public concern over the question of prison security in general. A comfortable interpretation, more plausible though, is Crossman's thesis that the Conservative Party were hoping to make another 'security scandal' out of Blake's escape by linking it with the Russians.[62] Roy Jenkins was anxious to avoid this, and to prevent concentrated fishing in such muddy and politically embarrassing waters he widened Mountbatten's brief. A deft and successful manoeuvre in political terms, but clearly a disastrous one for the prison service and it is difficult to believe that Hugh Klare could have left the Howard League in 1971 in anything other than a pessimistic mood. For twenty years he had worked closely with the prison service, at all levels, even to the extent of trying to pacify its more militant critics such as those imprisoned campaigners for nuclear disarmament. It must have been sad for Klare to reflect that the rehabilitative ideal which he had sought to bring to the prison service had been so rudely circumscribed in the cause of political expediency.

The Howard League's emphasis on the prison system should not obscure its efforts to secure alternatives to imprisonment. This is an important point to stress since there is a widespread impression in the penal lobby that the League has said almost nothing about alternatives over the years. Such an impression is totally false. As early as 1955, the League raised the possibility of the suspended sentence and also canvassed the idea of adult attendance centres. The suspended sentence had first been raised by Sir Leo Page who believed that many probationers did not always understand that they could be punished for their original offence if they committed a further offence while on probation. He felt that if an actual sentence was passed, but suspended, the probationer would have a much clearer idea about where he stood. The League presumably felt that such a sentence would strengthen probation and therefore encourage its wider use by magistrates instead of imprisonment. The Advisory Council on the Treatment of Offenders was not so convinced and it reported against the suspended sentence in connection with probation, or otherwise, in very blunt terms in 1952.[63] By raising the possibility again so soon after the Council's report the League was in danger of straining its credibility and it was wisely decided to drop the matter in preference for other alternatives, in particular, adult attendance centres.[64]

To look back on adult attendance centres as they were envisaged by the Howard League in the mid 1950s is not pleasant; their rationale was strictly punitive and the proposal that offenders should sew mailbags was justified on the grounds that it should show them how much society disapproved of their actions. No doubt this disapproval would be reinforced by the retired prison warders and policemen who were to run the centres.[65] If this was a time when alternatives to short term imprisonment had to be seen to be tough then the League fully met this requirement by suggesting a regime almost totally at odds with its much vaunted rehabilitative ideal. How this contrasts with the positive proposals it was later to support, as advocated by Philip Priestley in his paper on Day Training Centres as an alternative to short term imprisonment, is a good example of how far the penal lobby had travelled in just over a decade.[66]

Priestley's case was a strong one. Short term prisoners share a number of characteristics: fragmented work records, broken or difficult family backgrounds and a general incapacity to deal with what most would regard as fairly routine social responsibilities. To imprison such people for short periods is almost totally useless. There is no time for any serious attempt at rehabilitation and as likely as not the offender is back inside within a couple of months. This is not only unhelpful to the offender, it is also an unnecessary burden on the penal system. Dealing with short term prisoners takes up two-thirds or more of the administrative time of local prison staffs who have to go through the laborious process of reception and discharge at very short intervals.

The alternative put forward by Priestley was that instead of sentencing offenders for short terms of imprisonment they should be given probation on the condition that they attend a non-residential day training centre. These centres would be staffed by psychologists and/or social workers who would devise suitable programmes to help each offender overcome his personal or vocational difficulties. The help of outside agencies would be encouraged, to teach offenders how to read and write or perhaps to upgrade their work skills.

Similar proposals came from other sources and eventually the Home Office was persuaded to provide for Day Training Centres in the Criminal Justice Act (1972). Although the Howard League played only a very modest part in this process of persuasion, there is no denying that by this time its commitment to the idea of progressive alternatives to short term imprisonment was visible and firm.[67] In a slightly different context, though very much about alternatives, the League came out strongly in the 1970s in favour of reforming bail procedures. To deny a person his liberty is rightly regarded by most people as a very serious step. Yet it is just this step which is taken with almost reckless abandon by magistrates when refusing to grant bail. In 1970, for example, the number of untried persons in custody was 47,225: 21,103 of these did not return to prison on conviction and 2,472 were acquitted. These figures indicate a degree of hardship, not to say injustice, which the Howard League found unacceptable, and its published evidence to the Home Office on granting bail in magistrates' courts expressed this concern in plain language and called for the following two principles to be embodied in law and in practice:

(1) That unless it can be established, with specific reasons, that there is a real danger that the accused will not attend his trial then, with certain closely defined exceptions, bail should normally be granted. The onus should not be on the defendant to ask for it.
(2) That the decision whether to deprive a man of his liberty should never be made unless all the available relevant information about him has been considered by the Court.[68]

The significance of these two principles is obvious; if implemented they would redefine bail procedures firmly in favour of the accused. Those who felt that this was going too far were reminded that many people are remanded in custody without ever asking for bail simply because they are ignorant that this is their right. To reinforce this point the League made a specific recommendation that, subject to means, legal aid should be explicitly offered to anyone in danger of being placed in custody. The problem as it affects the young is particularly ironic. The League felt that it was strange that successive governments sought to keep young offenders out of prison at all costs, yet at the same time was prepared to sanction a system which committed hundreds of untried young people to prison or remand centres. This can only increase the young person's sense of alienation and, in certain cases, deliver him into the hands of the more experienced offender. The imprisonment of girls on remand in Holloway is particularly undesirable and the League rammed this message home by drawing on the researches of one of its leading members, and Britain's first professor of forensic psychiatry, T.C.N. Gibbens.[69]

Because of its obvious inadequacies the granting of bail in magistrates' courts was an easy target for attack. Criticism had been strident for several years and more than one organisation had argued for alternative systems. It was on these alternatives that the Howard League placed much emphasis, referring in some detail to the Vera Bail Project. Briefly, this project was started in Manhattan during 1961, and operates on the principle that the accused is more likely to appear for trial if he has his roots in the local community. To evaluate this community identity the accused is asked a number of questions about his family ties, work patterns and so on. Project workers then simply translate these answers into a points score which indicates to the Court whether or not he is a good risk. The early results of this carefully monitored project were impressive. Of those 2,300 recommended by project staff for bail in the first thirty months, 99 per cent returned to Court when the law required.[70] The advantages of this scheme are considerable. Not only does it eradicate the problem of sureties, it also works against the practice of punitive remands whereby hardline magistrates, quite illegally, deny bail in order that the accused can either 'cool off' or have 'a taste of prison'.

Coupled with this alternative the provision of bail hostels was also recommended. This was of some importance since although there are many reasons why magistrates deny bail, by far the commonest reason given is that the accused has no fixed abode. The fact that many accused people are living with friends or in a hostel is not normally accepted as evidence of secure accommodation. The Howard League felt quite rightly that to place such people in prison because they were allegedly homeless according to this definition is unjust, and even where homelessness can be proved the accused should be referred to newly created bail hostels and not remanded to prison.

Although this summary of the Howard League's evidence is far from complete, its concern to change the way of granting bail in magistrates' courts in a progressive direction can hardly be a matter of dispute. True, many of its suggestions had been previously put forward by other organisations. But this is not to deny that the League showed itself willing enough to argue for alternatives to the rising army of people on custodial remand. However, the same wholehearted commitment does not seem to have been so evident in its response to the Advisory Council's report, *Young Adult Offenders* (1974). But even in this case it is possible to urge that the League's position was far more progressive than it would at first appear.

The Advisory Council's report can only be described as a thoroughly contradictory document. It began by accepting that there is no evidence that custodial treatment is more effective than non-custodial treatment, and that although non-custodial methods have not been proved to be more successful, the Council believed that 'the goal of assisting the offender to lead his life and manage his affairs without committing an offence has a better change of being achieved in the community than by committing him to custody'.[71] Yet, having made this bold declaration, the Council went on to produce a report which even some of its own members regarded as showing an excessive preoccupation with custodial treatment, requiring a new and punitive role for the probation service against which many of its younger members actively campaigned.[72] At one stage it looked as though the probation service might jettison the Advisory Council's report in its entirety. The Howard League, on the other hand, accepted the report on the basis that:

> As regards the main philosophy and proposals of the Report, we recognise that in some ways it is a compromise: several members of the Advisory Council signed it with reservations, and we hope that the various sections of public and professional opinion who also have reservations will similarly support it as a basis for progress. It would be in no one's best interest to demand a completely new start at this stage; nor to drift along with the *status quo ante*.[73]

This pragmatic, almost bland, response should not be taken to mean that the League fully supported the report's custodial emphasis. It did not; on the contrary, it was openly critical of this emphasis and made several detailed criticisms. Further, where the Council had allowed for non-custodial treatment the League worked hard to make sure that these proposals would be interpreted in a new and imaginative way. Combine this with its position on day training centres and bail and there is clear evidence of the League's commitment to alternatives.

Whether this commitment was too narrowly conceived, or too cautiously advocated, are legitimate questions which remain to be answered. Whatever the answers though, it is a caricature of the League's position in the 1970s to argue that it somehow totally ignored the value of alternatives.

If prison sentences cannot be avoided, and offenders have to serve time, then the Howard League has always fought to ensure that on release suitable after-care agencies are available to help offenders in the difficult task of readjusting to the community. Exactly how these after-care agencies should be structured has not often been agreed, nor has their operation always been satisfactory. It was against this background, and the passing of the Criminal Justice Act (1948) which made new statutory demands in respect of after-care organised through the Central After-Care Association, that the government appointed a Departmental Committee on Discharged Prisoners' Aid Societies in 1951. In its evidence to this Committee, and concentrating on non-statutory after-care, the Howard League made two important suggestions. First, it argued that after-care should begin during imprisonment and should be carried out by newly-created Prison Rehabilitation Officers who, as experienced social workers, would assess the offender's needs and make preparations for his release. Such officers would be part of the prison service and liaise with the Discharged Prisoners' Aid Societies which would operate outside of prisons in a more or less auxiliary role to the new and professional rehabilitation service. Second, the League also envisaged, either through a scheme of attachment to prisoners' wages or, more simply, the arrival of the welfare state, that the Discharged Prisoners' Aid Societies would no longer have to provide 'tide-over' money on release, thus allowing their many voluntary workers to develop their role, not as material providers, but as family counsellors and friends. That the League's evidence was in tune with government thinking can be shown by reference to the White Paper, *Penal Practice in a Changing Society,* which summarised the Departmental Committee's evidence to mean that:

> Aid Societies should reduce the emphasis they had traditionally placed on immediate material aid and develop and deepen their interest in meeting the individual needs of selected prisoners not subject to statutory after-care. To assist the societies, the Committee proposed that well qualified Prison Welfare Officers should be appointed at local prisons as employees of the National Association of Discharged Prisoners' Aid Societies. At the present time eight of these new Prison Welfare Officers have been

appointed at five prisons, and it is hoped that their services will be extended to all local prisons as soon as possible. With their cooperation, the local Aid Societies must be encouraged to seek new ways to deepen and widen their new task of assisting the social rehabilitation of those who need and can profit by their help. (para 82)

True, the League did not get exactly the structure it had outlined in its evidence, but the Departmental Committee's recommendations on non-statutory after-care were near enough to its own proposals for the League to endorse them with obvious satisfaction. [74]

The League continued to take an interest in after-care and was particularly keen to increase the number of Prison Welfare Officers, and also to improve their status and qualifications. (This was all part of Hugh Klare's grand design to professionalise the entire prison service.) Some improvements on this front can be traced, but they were initially very modest, and this, no doubt, reflects the uneasy progress of the dual, statutory and non-statutory after-care service as it limped into the sixties. It was in an effort to devise a more rational and efficient system that the government referred the whole question of after-care to the Advisory Committee on the Treatment of Offenders which reported in October 1963. Briefly, the Report recommended that statutory and non-statutory after-care should be merged into one service, and to cope with what would be an increasingly heavy workload the probation service should be expanded and reorganised as the Probation and After-Care Service. The League put forward several useful ideas to the Advisory Council, such as the need for the Discharged Prisoners' Aid Societies to provide more hostel accommodation. In general though, the League's evidence was not as tightly drawn and it compares very unfavourably with its earlier contribution to the Departmental Committee in 1951. Perhaps the League's most valuable contribution to the welfare of ex-offenders was yet to come, namely, its part in promoting the Rehabilitation of Offenders Act. A detailed look at how this Act came into being reveals not only the persistence of the penal lobby, it also shows the Howard League continuing to move with assurance through the politico-legal establishment.

The Howard League has often been associated with moves to rehabilitate offenders by expunging their criminal records after a suitable lapse of time. As early as 1954, for example, Hermann Mannheim pressed the League's Executive Committee to look into the matter and suggested a joint meeting between the League and the ISTD for that purpose. [75] This particular initiative seems to have come to nothing, and even when the subject was raised again in more detail during the summer of 1962 the outcome was no more encouraging.[76] A formal request for government action in the shape of the League's evidence to an ACTO enquiry into non-custodial penalties and disabilities also drew a blank in the mid 1960s. Undeterred the League took up the subject yet again in 1969 when it approached the Criminal Department at the Home Office in the very modest context of expunging the record of a first offence after ten or fifteen years.[77] The Home Office response to this approach is not available in any detail, but it seems fairly obvious that although it was not in principle hostile to reform along these lines, it was certainly not prepared to take the initiative, apart from the necessary polite promise 'to go into the matter further'. The subject might well have rested there had not the Howard League been joined by Justice and the National Association for the Care and Resettlement of Offenders (NACRO). These two organisations lent their prestige to the League's call for reform, and also joined it in setting up a Working Party on Previous Convictions which held its first meeting in December 1970.[78] The composition of the Working Party is of some interest. The chairman was Lord Gardiner, a leading light in Justice, and also a long standing member of the Howard League. The Working Party also included a Queen's Counsel, Louis Blom-Cooper, shortly to become chairman of the Howard League, and two barristers, one being Paul Sieghart who eventually wrote the Working Party's final report. Two stipendary magistrates and a solicitor were also included and Mrs Kate Frankl, JP, participated as the only woman member of the Working Party. Hugh Klare from the Howard League and Tom Sargant and Henry Hodge from Justice gave the Working Party additional grit in that all three were experienced campaigners in the closely-knit fabric of legal politics.[79]

The Working Party quickly set to work and at its very first meeting decided that even if the Home Office was not intending to take any initiative itself, it must at the very least have some views about the possibilities of expunging old convictions and the lines that any future legislation would probably have to follow. With this in mind the Howard League arranged for an informal meeting between the Working Party and a senior civil servant to sort out what the Home Office would be likely to accept and, more important, what it would oppose. Although this meeting was useful, the Home Office remained unenthusiastic. To what extent this was the result of a directive from the newly-appointed Conservative Minister remains an open question. On balance, the available evidence points more firmly towards civil service opinion which anticipated that expunging old convictions would be very awkward to formulate into a sensible and practical scheme. This negative thinking, combined with the very real difficulty of more pressing government business, is probably the best explanation of why the Home Office tried to keep its distance. In any event, the Working Party must soon have realised that if its final report was to persuade the ministry it would need to be well researched and thoroughly practical.

With this in mind the Working Party began a detailed enquiry into the problem of old convictions in other countries which pointed towards the isolation of the United Kingdom. The Working Party's report was eventually able to claim that 'our country is the only member of the Council of Europe without a law by which a man's rehabilitation can be accepted by society'.[80] This was obviously a useful comparative dimension in the argument for reform.

Equally helpful to the Working Party's case was the estimate that there were about one million people in England and Wales with a criminal record more than ten years old.[81] That is, there are about a million people in England and Wales who, according to official figures at least, had gone straight for a period of at least ten years and yet whose criminal records were still kept and whose old convictions were still regarded in certain circumstances as reason enough for discriminatory action. The possible availability of an estimate along these lines was first discussed by the Working Party in May 1971. The Home Office was subsequently approached, but its initial response was not encouraging. Doubts were expressed about whether the Research Unit could produce such an estimate, even if the necessary time was made available. This massively unhelpful attitude was fortunately side-stepped and by December 1971 the Research Unit had produced the relevant figures and even found time to comment on the Working Party's draft report.

This statistical information was obviously essential, but by itself it did little to illustrate in any vivid sense why the United Kingdom's reluctance to expunge old convictions caused so much personal hardship. To get this across, which the Working Party quite rightly felt was crucial, it was agreed that the published report should begin with a number of case histories, each carefully chosen to show the plight of the reformed and respectable citizen trying to live down a past conviction.[82]

This human interest aside, the Working Party had to make up its mind on a number of other important issues. First, if it was recommended that old convictions should be expunged after a certain period had elapsed, in which the offender had gone straight and shown himself rehabilitated, did this mean that his criminal record would then be destroyed or perhaps sealed up at the Criminal Record Office and access denied to it for any purpose? The Working Party came out firmly against destruction or even the sealing-up of records on the somewhat lofty basis that criminological research in this country is still in its infancy and bodies like the Cambridge Institute of Criminology and the Home Office Research Unit should not be denied any information which might further our understanding of crime. On a more pragmatic level, the Working Party moved positively to meet what they already knew to be the government's anxiety over access for other public agencies by recommending that the police and other public authorities working in areas of known social risk, e.g. the employment of schoolmasters, the licensing of child care establishments, should also have access to all official records, even those of rehabilitated offenders. The courts were also to have all available information if a rehabilitated offender was later to be convicted of a serious offence.[83]

Having anticipated possible government objections over access the Working Party went on to recommend what some of its members felt to be unnecessarily long periods of rehabilitation:

(1) Five years where no custodial sentence was imposed on conviction.
(2) Seven years where a custodial sentence of not more than six months was imposed.
(3) Ten years where a custodial sentence of not more than two years was imposed.

The simple fact that rehabilitation was not considered for offenders receiving custodial sentences of more than two years is an indication of the Working Party's over-cautious approach. This timidity was justified by a felt need to placate public opinion.

The gist of the Working Party's recommendations was to create a new social category – rehabilitated offenders. That is, members of our community who, though once fairly and openly convicted in Court, could after the required period of rehabilitation make a lawful declaration, say in a job application, claiming to have no previous convictions. Any evidence to the contrary in a Court of Law would, with very few exceptions, be inadmissible. Once the scope of the Working Party's recommendations are fully understood, the reluctance of the Home Office to take up the problem of old convictions may seem more understandable. A number of powerful interests were directly affected, and to ensure that any legislative proposals had the backing of at least some of these interests would not be easy. The reaction of insurance companies and employers is a case in point. Many firms block bond their employees to cover losses caused by dishonesty.[84] This form of bonding can be voided by an insurance company if it is discovered that one of the firm's employees has a criminal record. Under the Working Party's proposals insurance companies would not, in the case of rehabilitated offenders, have much chance of winning any legal action on that ground alone. Considerations like these led to informal contacts between insurance company representatives and members of the Working Party during the summer of 1971. On this and allied issues Lord Gardiner also met a CBI committee which had been especially formed to look into what problems might arise for industry if the Working Party was gratified.

One of the most impressive things about the Working Party was its ability to make all these contacts within so short a time. By February 1972 its Report was published and, in anticipation of the Home Office's reluctance to take up its recommendations, a draft bill was also well on the way to completion. It was this bill, the Rehabilitation of Offenders Bill, that Lord Gardiner eventually introduced into the House of Lords just before the Christmas recess in 1972. After the formal First Reading it was discussed in principle during February 1973 and in putting the case for the Bill, Lord Gardiner showed considerable tactical skill. Speaking for the government Lord Colville was in favour of the broad objectives of the Bill but then, after going out of his way to speak at length on a number of trivial objections, he picked on one really sensitive issue, defamation. He commented:

> In defamation . . . we have a main pivot of the Bill, because it is upon the frightening effect of possible defamation suits that I think many of the changes in the public attitude which the noble and learned Lord wants will turn. In this country defamation traditionally carries with it the defence that what was said is true.[85]

As we have already pointed out, in certain circumstances the Working Party was prepared to jettison this defence, and it was this aspect of the Rehabilitation of Offenders Bill that Lord Colville found so undesirable. Apart from this technical problem over the law on defamation there was also a certain feeling of unease that allowing a rehabilitated person to deny his previous convictions was tantamount to providing him with a licence to lie.

When the Bill returned to the floor of the House for more detailed scrutiny most of the exchanges that really mattered focussed on these same points and Lord Colville, who knew that the Bill had virtually no chance of succeeding, finally declared the government's hand by stating that he did not feel that anything should be put into the Bill which ran counter to what the Faulks Committee might have in mind. This was crucial since not only was the Faulks Committee on Defamation a long way from completing its enquiry, it was known to be hostile to the Bill which it had already seen in draft form. Thus, when Lord Gardiner later expressed the hope, during the Bill's Third Reading, that the government would take over the new measure in the Commons, he knew that this was highly unlikely. It came as no surprise therefore when the Bill lapsed at the end of the Parliamentary session.

We now enter a phase in which the beneficiaries of the Working Party's report, those people with old convictions, were virtually overlooked in the internecine struggle between rival groups in the legal establishment. The report's recommendations, with the full support of a former Lord Chancellor, cut sharply across traditional views about the law relating to libel. The Faulks Committee with its own phalanx of legal experts was opposed to these recommendations. In the closely knit legal establishment opinion and personalities divided as the debate spilled over from the Inns of Court to Parliament.

The Working Party's Bill, now amended to include offenders with a previous custodial sentence of up to thirty months instead of two years, had been thoroughly debated in the Lords. Given the government's reluctance, there was now only one way forward, a Private Member's Bill in the House of Commons. The Bill's supporters were fortunate in securing the help of Mr Kenneth Marks who, although low in the ballot, contrived with the help of the Working Party to introduce the Rehabilitation of Offenders Bill with Alex Lyon as one of its sponsors early in 1974. The Second Reading debate was restrained, except perhaps for the magistrates lobby which argued strongly that information about offenders' past convictions should always be made available to magistrates as an indispensible aid to sentencing.[86] But this issue apart, there was little to raise the temperature. Mark Carlisle, the Minister of State at the Home Office, made it clear that in many ways he approved of the Bill. He also acknowledged its crossbench support, but he could not help but tell the House that he had been written to by Mr Justice Faulks. This by itself was enough to put the Bill's future in doubt and the 'Miners' Election' probably saved the government from throwing out a controversial Bill which it was not prepared to struggle with during the tense political winter of 1974.

With this legislation already in progress, and no doubt guarding against the future as well, the Faulks Committee did more than just write to Mark Carlisle. By March 1974 it had prepared and published a ten page interim report. In essence, and in form, the report was a direct attack on the Working Party's proposals. Names were named, and the argument blunt. The effects of Lord Gardiner's and Mr Marks' Bill would be unacceptable because:

> In principle we view with disfavour the creation by this Bill of a special class of person about whom the truth cannot safely be told after a specified period. We think it is in the public interest that truth should at all times remain a defence to actions for defamation. It is in our view wrong in principle that a man about whom the truth is told should be entitled to damages on that account. Where it is unfair and not in the public interest to tell the truth about a person the publisher can be charged with criminal libel. [87]

In the face of this critical challenge it is difficult not to believe that the Bill to rehabilitate offenders would have failed to get through Parliament had it not been for the return of a Labour Government after the 'Miners' Election'. Moreover, it was a Labour Government with Alex Lyon as a Minister of State at the Home Office. Having sponsored the Bill by Kenneth Marks he was under some obligation to continue his support, whatever arguments were put to him by the conservative wing of the legal establishment. With this in mind the Working Party was quick to find another backbencher to pilot their Bill through the private members' procedure. The MP, interestingly, was a West Country Tory, Mr Piers Dixon.

In his first statement on the reintroduced Bill, Alex Lyon made his position clear. The reservations expressed by the Faulks Committee in its interim report were unacceptable:

> I must raise one issue of principle that has been voiced by the Committee on Defamation under Mr Justice Faulks which will require a good deal of discussion in committee. Mr Justice Faulks' committee is concerned about the Bill and particularly the section on defamation. He and the committee believe that it is wrong in principle that when a person states the truth about another person he should be liable in defamation merely because an Act of Parliament says that the truth has no effect. This is the material and, indeed, crucial issue in the Bill.
>
> Mr Justice Faulks and his committee recommend that for that reason, and apart from some technical matters that . . . the clause

on defamation should be omitted. If it were so the Bill would be without meaning. If it were the case that, though a man was not bound to disclose when asked about a previous conviction which had become spent, someone else could disclose it . . . no protection would be given by the Bill.

We must consider the issue of principle. Is it right that in this community what has been true in the sense that a man has been convicted should be regarded for all practical purposes as untrue? I think that is right. I take the view that truth is not any more paramount than any other principle of civilised conduct in civilised society. There is also compassion and understanding. For that reason we must balance compassion and understanding against a declaration of truth. I think that Mr Justice Faulks' committee underestimated the concern there is in society about this area of difficulty.[88]

With this firm statement the passage of the Bill was secure, but there were still necessary compromises to make and more than one anxious moment. In the first place, the Lords inserted an amendment which meant that the plaintiff, that is the rehabilitated person, would have to prove in any action he brought for defamation that the defendant in disclosing details about his past convictions had been malicious. This was placing the onus squarely on the rehabilitated person, an amendment which the Minister of State had to accept as the best compromise he could get in the face of continued opposition to the Bill which by this time had been taken up in the columns of *The Times.* The deal worked out with the Magistrates' Association, allowing its members access to information about spent convictions, was less damaging to the spirit of the Bill but, again, a reluctant compromise.

The pressure exerted by supporters of the Faulks Committee in both Houses continued to be considerable, and the Bill's Tory opponents from the legal establishment were only finally isolated by the support given to the Bill by the Conservative Party's backbench committee on Home Affairs.[89] Ironically though, it could be argued that the main threat to the Bill came from Alex Lyon himself who at one stage offered to take over the measure and bring it forward as government legislation. The Working Party presumably felt that, in spite of his commitment to the Bill, the minister simply did not have enough political clout to ensure that it would get through in what might be a short Parliament. For this reason, correctly as things turned out, the Minister's offer was rejected.[90]

The Working Party's success owed much to persistence. With the legal establishment divided, opposition to its recommendations was fierce from the very start. But it required expertise as well as staying power. Technical amendments had to be drafted for Parliament and the strength of moral and legal arguments of public figures like Lord Hailsham met with equal intellectual force. It is difficult to think of any groups better placed to provide this expertise than the Howard League, Justice and NACRO. All have tough-minded supporters on the liberal wing of the legal establishment. Moreover, these supporters, either through personal contacts or overlapping membership, were able to work both Parliament and the bureaucracy with a quiet but sure touch, even when the going was tough. The Howard League is very much at home in such a legally orientated and well-connected lobby, even if on this occasion its detailed contribution was unquestionably second to that of Justice.

This synoptic appreciation of the Howard League has not, by definition, attempted to be exhaustive. Nothing, for example, has been said about the League's work through Margery Fry on the payment of compensation to victims who have suffered from crimes of violence, a contribution noted by Lord Butler in his White Paper on *Penal Practice in a Changing Society* (para 26). There are also a number of other areas where the League has attempted to make its influence felt, from the quality of the prison medical service to attachment of maintenance orders to wages. [91] Enough ground has been covered though, to indicate that a comprehensive survey of the League's evidence to various governmental and voluntary agencies would reveal a range of interests which is unparalleled in the penal lobby. It is the massive weight of this accumulated evidence that has contributed so readily to the Howard League's public reputation as a successful, perhaps even the most successful, pressure group in the ongoing struggle for a more liberal and enlightened penal policy. The great difficulty about accepting such an assessment is that public reputations can so quickly become public cliches. It is, therefore, even as part of a conventional critique, worth considering whether this reputation is justified, and also perhaps raising the possibility that the League's achievements have been limited by an over-close association with the bureaucracy and, in particular, those officials who are directly concerned with operating the penal system.

NOTES

[1] As a matter of interest the Howard Association actually campaigned against the central ownership and control of local prisons

at the time, fearing that it might lead to a prison system closed to independent local scrutiny. This fear was by no means unfounded.
[2] Gordon Rose, *The Struggle for Penal Reform,* Stevens, London, 1961, p.30. My emphasis.
[3] Gordon Rose, *The Struggle for Penal Reform,* Stevens, London, 1961, chapter 3.
[4] Gordon Rose, *The Struggle for Penal Reform,* Stevens, London, 1961, p.46.
[5] Gordon Rose, *The Struggle for Penal Reform,* Stevens, London, 1961, p.49.
[6] Gordon Rose, *The Struggle for Penal Reform,* Stevens, London, 1961, p.60.
[7] Gordon Rose, *The Struggle for Penal Reform,* Stevens, London, 1961, p.65.
[8] Tallack was not allowed to retire in peace. As late as 1907 the Humanitarian League recalled, with obvious relish, his long opposition to the newly established Court of Criminal Appeal, a reform which the League had pressed for over many years. *(The Humanitarian,* vol. III, no.69, November 1907.)
[9] Sheila Rowbotham, *Hidden from History,* Pluto Press, London, 1974, p.85.
[10] In July 1913, for example, the League spoke out strongly against the Cat and Mouse Act *(Quarterly Record,* vol.5, no.3, July 1913, p.4) and a year later roundly condemned the forcible feeding of a militant suffragette as 'intolerable and as such as nothing could justify'. (*Quarterly Record,* vol.VI, no.2, April 1914, p.10).
[11] Gordon Rose, *The Struggle for Penal Reform,* Stevens, London, 1961, p.75.
[12] Gordon Rose, *The Struggle for Penal Reform,* Stevens, London, 1961, p.108.
[13] Enid Huws Jones, *Margery Fry,* Oxford University Press, London, 1961, p.113. Fenner Brockway associated himself with the Penal Reform League rather than the Howard Association because he thought that the former was more radical.
[14] Gordon Rose, *The Struggle for Penal Reform,* Stevens, London, 1961, p.97.
[15] Gordon Rose, *The Struggle for Penal Reform,* Stevens, London, 1961, p.110. Stephen Hobhouse in contrast seems to suggest a more direct relationship between the publication of the Report and subsequent reforms. See Stephen Hobhouse, *Forty Years and An Epilogue,* James Clarke, London, 1951, pp.178 and 179.
[16] Gordon Rose, *The Struggle for Penal Reform,* Stevens, London, 1961, p.172. The League's part in this reform is also acknowledged

by J.E. Hall-Williams, *The English Penal System in Transition*, Butterworth, London, 1976, p.146.
[17] Gordon Rose, *The Struggle for Penal Reform*, Stevens, London, 1961. See chapter 10 for a full account of the League's activities in this field.
[18] Gordon Rose, *The Struggle for Penal Reform*, Stevens, London, 1961, p.160.
[19] For example, Margery Fry persuaded Cyril Burt to write a pamphlet on *The Psychology of the Young Criminal* which was published by the Howard League in 1924. (The credibility of Cyril Burt's research on the young delinquent has recently been called into question by Jack Tizard, Professor of Child Development at London University.) M. Hamblin Smith, author of *The Psychology of the Criminal*, also contributed two articles to the Howard Journal in the early twenties.
[20] Gordon Rose, *The Struggle for Penal Reform*, Stevens, London, 1961, p.224.
[21] As Margery Fry put it in a family note, 'I'm afraid wire-pulling is what I'm really born for, but if the bell rings at the end of the pulls it seems worthwhile.' This assessment was made in the context of an interview with Sir George Newman about the Prison Medical Service. Enid Huws Jones, *Margery Fry*, Oxford University Press, London, 1961, p.115.
[22] Gordon Rose, *The Struggle for Penal Reform*, Stevens, London, 1961, p.225.
[23] *Penal Practice in a Changing Society*, February 1959, HMSO, London, Cmnd.645, p.1.
[24] For a general assessment of the League's attitude towards the Criminal Justice Act (1948) see, HLPR, *Annual Report*, 1947–48, pp.3–5.
[25] HLPR, *Annual Report*, 1947–48, pp.4–5.
[26] HLPR, *Executive Committee Minutes*, January 1945.
[27] HLPR, *Executive Committee Minutes*, October 1958.
[28] *House of Commons Debates*, vol.412, cols.401–2.
[29] *House of Lords Debates*, vol.209, cols.107–8. The First Offenders Act (1958) was later repealed in the Criminal Justice Act (1972) and new provisions were enacted concerned with persons who had not been imprisoned before as opposed to first offenders. See section 20(1) and (2) of the Powers of Criminal Courts Act (1973).
[30] HLPR, *Executive Committee Minutes*, July 1947.
[31] HLPR, *Executive Committee Minutes*, October 1948.
[32] HLPR, *Executive Committee Minutes*, October 1955.
[33] HLPR, *Executive Committee Minutes*, October 1955. The

Howard League agreed to Gerald Gardiner serving on the National Campaign's Executive Committee as his name was then not so closely associated with the League as that of its secretary, Hugh Klare.
[34] J. Christoph, *Capital Punishment and British Politics,* Allen and Unwin, London, 1962, p.186.
[35] HLPR, *Executive Committee Minutes,* April 1961.
[36] *Howard Journal of Penology and Crime Prevention,* vol.13, no. 1, 1970, pp.4–5.
[37] *Howard Journal of Penology and Crime Prevention,* vol.13, no. 1, 1970.
[38] Leon Radzinowicz, *An Address to the Howard League,* Sevens, Cambridge, pp.15–16.
[39] R. Hood, *Crime, Criminology and Public Policy,* Heinemann, London, 1974, p.11.
[40] Leon Radzinowicz, *An Address to the Howard League,* Sevens, Cambridge, p.16.
[41] Quoted by Lord Butler, see R. Hood, *Crime, Criminology and Public Policy,* Heinemann, London, 1974, p.3.
[42] R. Hood, *Crime, Criminology and Public Policy,* Heinemann, London, 1974, p.15.
[43] Although the Home Office Research Unit dates officially from March 1957, Lodge claims that, in effect, it had been operating since September 1956. See Hood, *Crime, Criminology and Public Policy,* Heinemann, London, 1974, p.19.
[44] HMSO, *Penal Practice in a Changing Society,* February 1959, Cmnd.645, paragraph 21.
[45] Mr Butler was certainly well aware of their drawbacks. See Hood, *Crime, Criminology and Public Policy,* Heinemann, London, 1974, p.4.
[46] *The Guardian,* 11 December 1974, p.17.
[47] HLPR, *Executive Committee Minutes,* April 1962.
[48] HLPR, *Executive Committee Minutes,* November 1964.
[49] HLPR, *Executive Committee Minutes,* February 1966.
[50] HLPR, *Executive Committee Minutes,* September 1965.
[51] R. Hood, *Crime, Criminology and Public Policy,* Heinemann, London, 1974, p.417.
[52] HLPR, *Executive Committee Minutes,* July 1961.
[53] *Report of the Committee on Children and Young Persons,* HMSO, London, 1960, Cmnd.1191, p.1.
[54] Enid Huws Jones, *Margery Fry,* Oxford University Press, London, 1961, pp.237–8.
[55] HLPR, *Executive Committee Minutes,* November 1956.
[56] For this evidence see, HLPR, *Annual Report 1957–58,* pp.9–12.

[57] R. Hood, *Crime, Criminology and Public Policy*, Heinemann, London, 1974, pp.329–30.
[58] HLPR, *Executive Committee Minutes*, February 1968.
[59] The outside management consultants, and later the organisation and methods team from the Treasury, actually visited the League's office for discussions with Klare. See, HLPR, *Annual Review* 1967–68, p.3.
[60] The Longford Committee stressed this aspect of Klare's commitment. See *Crime, A Challenge to Us All*, Labour Party, London, 1964, p.49.
[61] For more details of the security measures, see J.E. Hall-Williams, *The English Penal System in Transition*, Butterworth, London, 1970, pp.96–7.
[62] R.H.S. Crossman, *The Diaries of a Cabinet Minister*, vol.2, Hamilton and Jonathan Cape, London, 1976, pp.89–90.
[63] HLPR, *Executive Committee Minutes*, April 1955.
[64] It is interesting, though, that the idea of the suspended sentence was again considered by the League, and not turned down completely, in 1962. (HLPR, *Executive Committee Minutes*, June 1962.) The government was eventually tempted, and the suspended sentence was introduced in the Criminal Justice Act (1967). On the available evidence Leon Radzinowicz was arguing by 1971 that it was a foreseeable failure (*Sunday Times*, 24 January 1971).
[65] HLPR, *Executive Committee Minutes*, October 1955.
[66] P. Priestley, *Day Training Centres: An Alternative to Short Term Imprisonment*, Howard League, London, 1970. Delivered to a conference organised by the Howard League on *Penal Policy at the Crossroads*.
[67] The League took a more generous view of its own contribution to the pressure for day training centres, at least by association. See, HLPR, *Annual Report*, 1971–72, p.4.
[68] *Granting Bail in Magistrates' Courts*, Howard League, London, 1972, p.18.
[69] *Granting Bail in Magistrates' Courts*, Howard League, London, 1972, pp.3–4.
[70] *Granting Bail in Magistrates' Courts*, Howard League, London, 1972, p.16.
[71] Quoted in a review of the Advisory Council's report, *Young Adult Offenders* (1974) by Radical Alternatives to Prison, part 1.
[72] This campaign had a significant impact on the National Association of Probation Officers' annual conference at Weymouth in May 1974.
[73] *Between Probation and Custody*, Howard League, London, 1975,

para A4. See also Martin Wright, 'Probation with Teeth', *Probation Journal,* vol.21, no.4, December 1974.
[74] HLPR, *Executive Committee Minutes,* July 1973.
[75] HLPR, *Executive Committee Minutes,* July 1954.
[76] HLPR, *Executive Committee Minutes,* June 1962.
[77] HLPR, *Council Minutes,* October 1969.
[78] HLPR, *Council Minutes,* November 1970.
[79] With Hugh Klare's departure to the Council of Europe his successor at the Howard League, Martin Wright, took over his duties as a member of the Working Party from late 1971.
[80] Justice, The Howard League and NACRO, *Living it Down: The Problem of Old Convictions,* Stevens, London, 1972, p.10.
[81] Justice, The Howard League and NACRO, *Living it Down: The Problem of Old Convictions,* Stevens, London, 1972, appendix C, pp. 42–3.
[82] Justice, The Howard League and NACRO, *Living it Down: The Problem of Old Convictions,* Stevens, London, 1972, pp.1–3.
[83] Justice, The Howard League and NACRO, *Living it Down: The Problems of Old Convictions,* Stevens, London, 1972, pp.11–12.
[84] For a discussion of this practice see, *Fidelity Bonds for Ex-Offenders,* Apex, London, 1971.
[85] *House of Lords Debates,* vol.338, col.747.
[86] The Bill was not generally popular with magistrates. An article in *Justice of the Peace* was later to ask, 'Why, we should ask ourselves, should it be thought necessary for press and public alike to be muzzled in this way? In particular, what is there in the nature of a criminal conviction which could justify such a perversion of the truth that is not present in any other aspect of a person's life?' *Justice of the Peace,* January 1974, p.138.
[87] *Interim Report of the Committee on Defamation,* HMSO, March 1974, Cmnd.5571, p.3.
[88] *House of Commons Debates,* vol.873, iss.no.964, cols.1546–7.
[89] In a bitter attack on the opponents of the Bill, a letter in *New Society* referred to 'the last-ditch campaign of the press and their lawyers, led by members of the official committee reviewing the law of defamation, to frustrate the Bill. The activities of this lobby would make an interesting case study of the way in which the press seeks to protect its interests at the expense of the community'. *New Society,* 1 August 1974, p.308.
[90] It is interesting to note that the effectiveness of the Rehabilitation of Offenders Act (1974) has recently been challenged. See Graham Zellick, 'Criminal Records', *The Sunday Times,* 3 October 1976, p.15.

[91] The League's international work has also been of considerable importance. Gordon Rose, *The Struggle for Penal Reform,* Stevens, London, 1961, pp.314–21.

4 The Howard League: a conventional and a radical critique

A conventional critique of the Howard League might well start from the inside by asking the following questions. First, what would the League itself regard as its outstanding successes since 1921 when it first came into being in its present form? Second, how has it seen its status *vis-a-vis* the bureaucracy in the continuing dialogue on matters of penal policy? And third, how does it see its future role and status?

On the question of successes, the League would claim to have exerted a direct and decisive influence in a number of important areas. For example, it has been argued that the League was directly responsible for the Poor Prisoners' Defence Act, 1930, the Summary Jurisdiction (Appeals) Act of 1933 and the scheme for prisoners' earnings. To these firm successes, already referred to in more detail, must be added the League's prominent part in the 1930s campaign against corporal punishment, and earlier, through Margery Fry's friendship with the Commissioners Waller and Paterson, the League's pressure to abolish the convict haircrop and the broad arrow in prison clothing. Since the war there have also been notable successes, the most obvious being George Benson's First Offenders Act (1958) and Margery Fry's suggestion for an Institute of Criminology. In association with Justice and NACRO, the passing of the Rehabilitation of Offenders Act (1974) also ranks as a considerable success for the League, to say nothing of its earlier role as the research base for the successful National Campaign for the Abolition of Capital Punishment.

This list of successes, compiled from Howard League publications, and from the published work of several of its most distinguished members, is not comprehensive. It is very considerable, though, and some political scientists would be reluctant, even in association with our synoptic appreciation, to take the list at its face value. However, starting out on the basis of appreciation and agreeing that in one way or another the Howard League has effected significant changes in penal policy over the years, we still need to ask why has it been so successful, how in the dialogue with the bureaucracy has it managed to achieve so much?

In the first place, the League would stress its reliance on facts, and the accuracy of those facts. Governments and their civil servants can be persuaded by reasoned argument supported by well researched evidence. But once a pressure group strays into idle speculation, and above all, inaccuracy, then all is lost. This was one of the reasons why the League kept the Prison Medical Reform Council at a safe distance and why it was not anxious to get involved with some of the wilder statements which came from certain members of the National Campaign for the Abolition of Capital Punishment. Associated with the League's emphasis on accuracy is the notion of civility. Civil servants holding sensitive posts in the Prison Commission are easy targets for unsympathetic abuse, but such abuse can turn out to be highly counter-productive. It is not possible to both abuse the prison service and then be invited to reform it. These twin notions of accuracy and civility have won for the League an unparalleled status *vis-a-vis* the bureaucracy. As Sir Lionel Fox, then Chairman of the Prison Commission, once put it:

> To start at the top on the national level I would first mention the position of the Howard League for Penal Reform . . . its existence . . . is recognised by authority as being, like that of 'His Majesty's Opposition' in the House of Commons, completely desirable and necessary. The Prison Commissioners are generally prepared to give the representatives of the Howard League full information and facilities to visit their establishments, and welcome their activity as a useful corrective to official complacency.[1]

This warm tribute was endorsed by R.A. Butler in a speech to the Howard League in November 1957 when he emphasised the 'well informed' nature of its criticisms, and also praised its efforts to come forward with 'constructive' suggestions. No other pressure group in the penal lobby has ever succeeded in winning quite such praise, or indeed, such access.

However, it would be quite wrong to deduce from this embrace that the Howard League never finds itself sharply at odds with the Home Secretary and/or his officials. This would amount to little more than a caricature of the relationship. There have been several occasions since the war when the League has spoken out aggressively against the Home Office. For example, it was widely believed that the Gowers Commission on capital punishment was being misled by the reluctance of some civil servants to argue against the 'departmental view', a situation which the Howard League found intolerable, arguing that:

> . . . the duty of the civil servant who can give useful and relevant evidence is to give it, and the duty of the 'Department' is to facilitate the giving of such evidence. Yet it is apparent that some able civil servants harbour the heresy that the 'Department' has a 'view', that this view (presumably of the higher ranks) must be sustained in public by those of the lower ranks whatever their personal opinions and experience. [2]

That such blunt criticism must have offended a number of senior civil servants is obvious. More recently, the joint statement issued by the League and NACRO on prison conditions was not exactly designed to endear either group to the then Home Secretary, James Callaghan.

These occasional outbursts, though, have failed to silence those critics who see the Howard League as being 'in the pocket of the Home Office', able perhaps to win certain useful reforms, but because of its close ties with the bureaucracy, unable to adopt the necessarily strident tactics which are sometimes needed in the struggle for penal progress. Criticism along these lines was current in the 1950s and it was discussed in depth at the League's Executive Committee meeting in June 1956. The Committee's reaction was perhaps predictable. Much of the discussion centred on publicity. It was argued that if the League was seen in such poor light it must be because its achievements and rationale were not widely enough known. Better publicity would soon put things right, and so there must be new pamphlets and a much more determined effort to work the media. As for being too close to the Prison Commission, well, certainly that was a danger and the League would have to guard against becoming the Commissioners' apologists. On the other hand, a close relationship with the Commissioners was essential for the League's success and should in no way be weakened. The meeting can be effectively summarised in the words of a member who commented that because

> so many people became emotional and sentimental about prison problems that a body like the League, careful in its statements and able to discuss prison problems knowledgeably with the Prison Commissioners, was essential. Its methods were sound, but an effort should be made to make its work more widely known. [3]

In an attempt to decide whether such monumental complacency was really justified, it might be as well to start by looking at a memorandum in defence of the Howard League's low profile which was circulated to the Executive Committee before its meeting.

In this memorandum it was argued that crime is a 'disorder of feeling' and therefore the problem of rehabilitation in how to change feelings. Prisoners often hate others because they hate themselves, an emotional hiatus which can only be put right by orchestrating their feelings in another way. This task is difficult enough to do at the best of times, in the present prison system it is almost impossible. The prisoner is continually put on the defensive by the ordinary prison officer who leads a dull and confined life in a hierarchic service modelled on military lines. Moreover, it is a service in which communication is limited and the frustrations of the ordinary officer regarded as of little consequence by the Governor or anyone else. In this situation it is no wonder that the officer will try to bolster up his status by demonstrating his superiority over the prisoners in his care. Indeed, he can only achieve some form of status at their expense. This realisation is the key to prison reform. Only when Governors can be persuaded to consult the ordinary officer, to give him a constructive role in an ongoing dialogue can we hope for prison officers with a purposeful and caring attitude towards rehabilitation.

Having identified the problem and provided a solution, on paper at least, the memorandum then went on to outline how far the League had progressed in trying to put the prison system right, how it had worked for a rapprochement between Governors and prison officers. The culmination of this progress was an invitation for the League's secretary to address the Governors at their annual conference, an invitation as it were to tell the Governors where they had gone wrong. This was the chance for a major breakthrough, and it had come about because of the League's style, its informed and constructive approach which had won the respect of an anxious and sensitive prison service. There was no sense in throwing this respect away by organising strident public campaigns which would only alienate the prison service and make it even more resistant to change. The Executive Committee member who prepared the memorandum summed up the position with characteristic honesty when he argued that, 'To surrender this relationship would surely be unwise; and if maintaining it is being called being in the pocket of the Prison Commission, then I plead guilty to this piece of acrobatics not without some sense of satisfaction.'

The Executive Committee was persuaded by the memorandum, but the question has to be asked, was it not misled? It is difficult not to believe that it was, in the very important sense that the justification for being in the Prison Commission's pocket was that great reforms were on the way in the prison service, reforms which would take it forward towards some great and shared rehabilitative ideal. If, in

1977, anyone really believes that this is what happened then it can only be a form of intellectual dishonesty. The tightening up of prison security after Mountbatten, the emergence of the Movement for the Preservation of the Rights of Prisoners (PROP), the prison riots of 1972 and the recent and brutal prison disturbance at Hull are evidence enough that the League's policy of remaining on close terms with those who run the prison service has, clearly, failed to produce the goods. Of course there have been gains here and there and, in fairness, as already pointed out, the League did speak out about the increase in prison security after Mountbatten. By then though, it was too late. Things might have been worse without the Howard League. A plausible argument, perhaps, but equally plausible is the radical thesis that the League's virtual colonisation by the prison service enabled the Home Office to put off reform on the basis that with the Howard League at its elbow it could at least appear to be doing something progressive. In this context too, the demand for more sweeping reforms put forward by other groups in the penal lobby could be judged extreme and defined out of court, at odds with responsible groups like the Howard League which were pressing the Home Office as far as it could possibly go in the face of a hostile public opinion. In this way the League was being used by the bureaucracy to cover its own inertia.

The Howard League has also been compromised by Home Office involvement with, and to some important extent control over, research. This is best illustrated by the League's attitude towards detention centres which were introduced under the provisions of the Criminal Justice Bill (1947). This Bill, as we have already seen, was drawn up in the 1930s, a period of penal optimism. At that stage there was no mention of detention centres, they were only to appear after the war and mainly in response to a rising crime rate. It is interesting to look back at the relevant Parliamentary papers to discover just how little debate there was over detention centres. It seems that the government had only a very crude idea about their purpose, namely, to give the young offender a short, sharp shock under a military style regime. There was no rehabilitative dimension; indeed, when objecting to an amendment which stressed educational provision, Chuter Ede felt that to emphasise education would only distract from the main purpose of the centres which was to provide 'a short, sharp punishment that will cause the young offender clearly to realise the injudiciousness of attempting continuously to flout the law. I want that part of the work to be clearly understood by all concerned.'[4] By 1954 two detention centres were in operation, one junior centre at Kidlington for fourteen to seventeen year olds, and another senior centre at Goudhurst in Kent for offenders between seventeen and twenty-one. The government felt certain that if effectively run, these centres could do much to contain juvenile delinquency and provide a suitable alternative to prison for offenders under twenty-one.

It was not long before the centres were being proclaimed a success, and further ones planned. This was announced in the 1959 White Paper, *Penal Practice in a Changing Society,* and a research study was quoted to reinforce the government's earlier optimism (para 33). Three months tough training appeared to be 'doing the lads some good'. This touching faith in detention centres was again evident during the passage of the Criminal Justice Bill (1961) when it became clear that the government intended to introduce a centre for girls, even though its Advisory Council on the Penal System had previously reported that this would not be practicable because the number of female offenders who might reasonably be sent to such a centre was too small. It was partly on this basis that Lord Stonham attacked the government's intention in the House of Lords, though his arguments, like those of Lady Wootton, had little effect and a detention centre for girls was subsequently opened at Moor Court in Staffordshire. The Lords debate did, however, succeed in once again focussing attention on the detention centre regime. What precisely were its objectives? Were they purely negative? Did it have to be so vigorous? Was there no alternative? These were all very pertinent questions in an atmosphere of growing suspicion. As Lord Longford said of detention centres in an unusually terse sentence, 'I believe that the truth has got about that they are pretty brutal establishments.'[5] Although such allegations had no immediate effect, and the number of detention centres increased after the Criminal Justice Act (1961), the system continued to attract very hostile criticism and by 1969 provision to abolish junior detention centres in favour of local authority controlled community homes was written into the Children and Young Persons Act of that year. The detention centre for girls at Moor Court had been declared unsuccessful by ACTO a year earlier in 1968.

The detention centre regime, both as it was originally conceived and indeed, as it came to be operated throughout the 1950s and 60s, was largely discredited by the late 1960s. The question remains then, where did the Howard League stand on this issue? In the 1940s it showed a certain degree of cautious ambivalence. Members of the Executive Committee were anxious over the provision of detention centres for children of school age, but also, and in common with many other activists in the penal lobby, they were not quite sure how detention centres could avoid developing into 'junior prisons'.[6] Yet, even allowing for these anxieties and doubts, and having received an assurance from the government that such centres would not be attached to prisons, the League was prepared to adopt a low profile, arguing that detention centres were unknown quantities and their development would have to be watched.[7]

This caution is not difficult to explain. The Criminal Justice Bill (1947) contained a provision to abolish corporal punishment as a sentence of the court. The League had long campaigned for this, and if detention centres were seen as the quid pro quo by the government faced with a rising juvenile crime rate, then they would have to be accepted, at least for the time being. Indeed, from a tactical point of view their inclusion might even have been regarded as a necessity. Further, if the regime did seem to be fairly tough this was not surprising so soon after the war and the experience of military service. Given time, detention centres might turn out to be far less punitive institutions than the government intended. Reasoning along these lines made it expedient for the League to 'wait and see'.

It turned out to be a very long wait, and even then it was left to an enterprising journalist from the *Daily Herald* to upstage the Howard League with two highly critical articles on what was happening at Kidlington and Goudhurst.[8]

Myrna Blumberg was clearly appalled by what she saw at both detention centres, and the first of her two articles appeared under the dramatic heading of, 'I call this BRUTAL'. Not only was the daily routine almost wholly negative, there were other even more worrying problems. For example, the selection of detainees seemed haphazard, no mental or physical certificates were required and therefore detainees ranged from the physically unwell to the seriously maladjusted. Could such young offenders really benefit from a 'short, sharp shock'? Moreover there was no aftercare; detainees were simply returned to the community with no more support than they had before.

It might be thought that *Daily Herald* readers would react against these criticisms, arguing that discipline never did anyone any harm, and that it was wrong to pamper young offenders. While it is certainly true that Myrna Blumberg was told by some readers to drop her 'sixth-form sentiment' and deal more firmly with these juvenile 'monsters', it is also true that she received a lot of support from readers who felt that detention centres hardened the young offender rather than reforming him.[9] Naturally, Miss Blumberg was not popular with the Prison Commissioners. In the first place they actually tried to ban her articles and when the *Daily Herald* refused to be bullied a statement from the Commissioners claimed that she had conveyed a fundamentally false impression about what was happening at detention centres, they were not 'brutalising' warehouses but institutions which, in that they deterred boys from crime, were turning out to be a very real success.

The Howard League was dismayed at the very thought of such a public quarrel. Several members of the Executive Committee had been approached by Miss Blumberg for their comments on detention centres, but mostly they had declined to offer any. It was against this unpromising background that Miss Blumberg agreed to attend the League's Executive Committee Meeting in November 1955. There is no doubt that every attempt was made to undermine the credibility of her reports. It was established that she had only been at Goudhurst for four hours, that she was not an expert in PT and that windows and doors were left unlocked at Kidlington where the atmosphere was generally better than at Goudhurst.[10] Why was Miss Blumberg given such a hostile reception? One thing is clear, it was not because the Howard League believed that detention centres were developing in a constructive direction. On the contrary, the League was opposed to their rigid discipline and the emphasis on physical training.[11] Indeed, Hugh Klare was quoted in the *Daily Herald* articles as arguing that 'The whole trend, at last, is towards constructive reform, whereas this goes right back.' Given this, the League's attitude mainly stemmed from what it regarded as an unhelpful public attack on the Prison Commissioners, on those very people whose goodwill was so essential in the pressure for reform. A familiar posture, but this was not the only reason for the League's anxiety as we shall see.

If Miss Blumberg's attack on detention centres did nothing else, it at least provoked the Howard League into action. It had failed to effectively monitor this new development in penal treatment and things were happening which needed to be put right, and in a hurry. It was then, with a sense of urgency that the League's Executive Committee drew up a list of suggested reforms early in 1956 and passed them on to the Prison Commission.[12] What the League looked for was a careful selection procedure to make sure that only the most appropriate boys were sent to detention centres. Sending the wrong type of offender had contributed to the present crisis. Further, the detention centre routine should be more constructive, social workers employed and aftercare made compulsory. In reply it is clear that the Commissioners were not unsympathetic over the insistence on more careful selection or indeed on the question of aftercare although they did point out that many boys already returned to statutory aftercare of one form or another. About the League's comments on the detention centre routine, the Commissioners were much less sympathetic, and it was clear that they were in no mood to recommend major changes. With this private exchange of views the League's active and critical interest in detention centres lapsed for several years until 1959 when it was announced that:

> In view of the encouraging results of detention centres, and the manifest desire of many courts to be able to use this form of treatment, it is proposed to accelerate the provision of more centres so that as soon as possible all sentences of six months or less may be of detention and not of imprisonment.[13]

Leaving aside the League's inherent unwillingness to provoke the Prison Commissioners, were there any other reasons why it held back on detention centres during this period, why it avoided a sustained effort to achieve a change of direction? A possible explanation is that corporal punishment was still very much an issue, soon to flare up in the Criminal Justice Bill (1960) and through the activities of the Anti-Violence League. In that detention centres remained for some people at least an acceptable alternative to corporal punishment the League continued to play a cautious game. This is plausible, but equally plausible is the explanation that the government's defence of detention centres, the research to which it was to refer again and again in the 1950s, and this included a specific reference in the White Paper quoted above, was carried out by Dr Max Grünhut, the Reader in Criminology at Oxford University and Executive Committee member of the Howard League.

Let it be clearly stated, we do not claim that Dr Grünhut's research was in any way inaccurate, though it is interesting that a different research design was later to give a much less optimistic view of detention centres.[14] However, it is being suggested that the Howard League's freedom of maneouvre over detention centres was very definitely limited by the fact that one of its own Executive Committee members had, on behalf of the government, carried out research which claimed that 'in terms both of reappearances in court and character improvement . . . the detention centre has a legitimate place in a variegated system of treatment for young offenders.'[15] For the League to have made a public and sustained attack on detention centres in these circumstances would have amounted to a vote of no confidence in one of its most distinguished academic members. The government had the League in a tight corner, and it did not hesitate to press home its advantage. Of course it might be argued that this should not be taken as an indictment of reforming academics who take on government research. After all, who was to say initially that Dr Grünhut's research might not have undermined the government's position on detention centres? This is certainly possible, but even this situation has its own constraints. Academic criminologists who are involved with penal reform groups are usually anxious, especially when their research is critical of government policy, to ensure that their work is used 'responsibly' by the groups with which they are identified. That this can blunt the edge of public criticism is obvious enough, but from the academic's point of view it is crucial, since even if he is not directly a recipient of government money an unsympathetic government can deny him many privileges, including access to penal institutions.[16] Very few academic criminologists of the traditional variety have been prepared to take such a risk, and therefore it is legitimate to suggest that their support for the Howard League has not always been the positive force that at first it might seem. This unwelcome fact should not obscure the fairly recent development of a research potential which is less directly funded by government, but even here the important problem of access remains.

Looking back over the League's early record on detention centres and, in particular, its very real efforts to build a much more humane and rehabilitative prison system it is difficult not to come to the conclusion that it was locked into the Prison Commission, and later the Prison Department, far too tightly for its own good.[17] This is not only because such a close relationship prevented the League from criticising the bureaucracy as often as it might have done, though this was indeed the case. More crucial though, is the realisation that the bureaucracy was charged with running an on-going system, one with a very strong institutional focus: its immediate concerns, therefore, were to monitor the progress of those institutions and to make suggestions for their better management and performance. In short, the bureaucracy was so preoccupied with the operational efficiency of the existing, institutionally orientated treatment paradigm that it was unable to conceive of treating the offender in any other than an institutional setting. The Howard League, by identifying so closely with the bureaucracy, by sharing in its day to day management concerns, suffered from much the same limitations and was consequently outflanked in the late 1960s and early 1970s by the movement for alternatives to imprisonment; that is, by the demand for a fundamental reappraisal of existing penal policy. This criticism is implicit in Martin Wright's frank article, 'Tactics of reform', written soon after he was appointed Director of the Howard League. About his immediate predecessors and their achievements, he writes:

> There can be many criticisms of all these innovations from today's vantage point, but in their time they were significant improvements. If reformers are to be criticised for their work in the 1950s and 1960s it should rather be for falling into the trap of concentrating too much on institutional practice, without enough questioning scrutiny of the underlying principles which should always be in the forefront of reformers' considerations. [18]

On the basis that what the League has always sought to do is to anticipate trends and hasten their development then in recent years it has partially failed. As the Howard Association once failed to anticipate the trend away from separate confinement so the League was not wholly aware of the strong and developing commitment to alternatives to imprisonment. This failure was by no means total, as we have tried in fairness to illustrate, and even the League's toughest critics must accept this qualification. But as we have written elsewhere, major changes in public policy are likely to be introduced in a gradual way. Resources have to be reallocated and the various publics persuaded that the changes involved are both necessary and possible.[19] In situations like this, a strident and firm commitment to new principles can help to polarise opinion, and with a mixture of luck and good judgement, speed up the process of change and reform. In the context of penal policy, the Howard League was not capable of taking this initiative in the late 1960s and early 1970s. This was the achievement of other pressure groups, most notably, Radical Alternatives to Prison.

Looking back it is perhaps to the League's credit that it responded so quickly to its critics, so much so that today its commitment to the search for alternatives to imprisonment is, for the most part, rarely questioned. This plus factor has to be balanced though, by the League's continuing courtship of the bureaucracy, a courtship which nearly turned into a marriage in 1975 when the League applied to the Voluntary Service Unit at the Home Office for a grant.[20] While it may well be that the Voluntary Service Unit is quite independent of the Prison, Probation and Criminal Departments at the Home Office, the League was surely naive to believe that this would not severely limit its freedom to criticise the bureaucracy. This application, which could almost be seen as an attempt to follow the absorbed Prison Commission into the Home Office, was turned down, and the League should be thankful. It is still far too closely linked with the bureaucracy through a network of advisory committees and personal contacts to wish back the days of its virtual colonisation by the Prison

Commission.

The League would probably argue that the risk of colonisation must always be the price of influence, and there is much sense in such an argument. The difficulty is that the League has traditionally functioned as a small, well connected, London based elite with no adequate democratic structures to limit this risk. There are no lively meetings where the Executive Committee has to justify its actions to a demanding membership. Quite the opposite, the Executive Committee can effectively do as it likes, and only very rarely does anyone raise the possibility that perhaps one or two of its members are out of touch with the drift of penal reform, or perhaps too closely allied with the establishment. It has happened, that is true. In 1974, for example, at the League's AGM, a member complained that the list of Council Members apparently came from *Who's Who* but criticism along these lines is rare. Indeed, criticism of any sort seems to have been regarded, traditionally at least, as somehow out of place. Members should be passive, leaving policy making to their betters, a way of conducting business which very much appealed to one Executive Committee member, Gordon Rose:

> Members write in or call now and again, raising points or giving information, some of them come to meetings or to the Summer School which is held every two years: some use the John Howard Library, which, however, is widely patronised by non-members also. There are no branches, although recently there has been a move to set up a Scottish section, and there are few occasions upon which the membership could influence the policy of the Executive. About the only way they could do this *en bloc* is at the Annual General Meeting, but it is rare for anyone to raise a point of any substance from the floor.
>
> In fact, the membership do not very much want to formulate the League's policy. What they want is a body of experts who are prepared to press upon the authorities an attitude of mind with which the membership in general agree. This, very roughly, is that the treatment of offenders should be primarily reformative in nature, rather than merely punitive . . . The details of how this is to be done, the membership is, by and large, prepared to leave to the officers and the Executive, rightly concluding that they should know what action to take.[21]

Such blatant elitism is difficult to justify, on any grounds, and to do the League justice things appear to be changing. The Scottish branch referred to was established, and there is now also a base in Wales. In addition to these national groups there is a well established county branch in Sussex and a new one in Devon. To help 'colonise' the rest of England as the Director phrased it, a Development Officer has recently been appointed, and this should help to increase the League's membership and improve its finances. Times for charities are hard, and this sensible move might guarantee the League's independence, thus saving it from ever again having to approach the Home Office for financial aid. But if the strategy stops here, if the membership drive is nothing more than a means to improve the League's finances then a valuable chance to democratise its structure will be lost. A substantial increase in membership, if it happens, would probably broaden the base of the League's membership, and lower the average age. Both these things are desirable, but such changes in themselves would do little to democraticise the League unless they are accompanied by a determined attempt to broaden the policy making process to somehow incorporate the regions and restrict the almost total autonomy of its London based Council.

The League's partial failure to anticipate new trends in penal reform in the late 1960s and early 1970s has led some critics to interpret this as part of a general and perhaps inevitable decline. The argument is that the League's aristocratic, socially well connected elite which once had such easy access to successive governments has been overtaken by the growth of professionalism and, in particular, the absorption of the Prison Commission into the Home Office. This thesis has been outlined by Terence Morris:

> Fifty years ago, after middle class suffragettes and conscientious objectors had been to prison . . . the penal reform movement gained considerable impetus. By mobilising influential figures of the political establishment such as the late Lord Templewood (the former Sir Samuel Hoare), an organisation like the Howard League became a voice that was taken seriously inside the Home Office. The sharing of a common social background gave the League, as it were, the inside track. Progressive prison commissioners such as Alexander Paterson and Lionel Fox looked to the League for support in ameliorating conditions that were the legacy of a Victorian prison system acknowledged in its day as one of the grimmest in Europe.
>
> But much has changed in the last ten years. The Prison Commission has been replaced by the Prison Department of the Home Office, and its critics would argue that by continuing in its old methods of Establishment diplomacy, the League has lost much of its fire. *(The Observer*, 27 August 1972.)

There is much evidence to support this view. The Howard League has to some extent faced a crisis of modernity; old methods were being applied to new and more complex patterns of decision making where personal contacts seem to matter less and less. However, it would be wrong to read into the Morris thesis the idea that somehow the League was effectively squeezed out of the penal lobby in the 1960s. Enough has been said to show that this was not so, the League was firmly locked into the bureaucracy during that decade, though it may well be that its union with the bureaucracy was changing in form and character. To put the same thing in a more concrete way, the Prison Commission was disbanded in 1963, and it was the League's chairman, Sir Kenneth Younger, who was appointed as Chairman of the newly formed Advisory Council on the Treatment of Offenders in 1966. This is not to suggest, of course, that the League's influence can ever be quite as immediate or direct as it was in the past. Apart from anything else, the penal lobby is now far too crowded for that. Equally, it would be silly of the Howard League's critics to believe that the League is somehow on its last legs. On the contrary, the League has come through a difficult period, but this has not seriously weakened the respect with which it is held by the bureaucracy, nor in any way lessened its faith in quiet persuasion based on well researched facts. The Howard League still has influence in the penal lobby.

Some of the more problematic features of the Howard League's way of operating have been noted, in one form or another, in other pressure group studies. Harry Eckstein, for example, pointed out that the BMA was not always as democratic as it might be; Self and Storing felt that the statutory embrace between the bureaucracy and the National Farmers' Union was perhaps a little too intimate; and M. Joel Barnett successfully demonstrated how a pressure group will stifle public criticism rather than upset a ministry on which it relies for public consultation and support.[22] To this extent, a *conventional* critique of the Howard League tells us little that is new about the relationship between second world pressure groups and government, and certainly it does little to expose the ideological assumptions on which that relationship is based. It is, in fact, only by developing a radical critique of the Howard League that a new dimension to this relationship begins to emerge and it is a dimension that takes us from the inside track of the Howard League to the less privileged environment of those pressure groups which belong, in Benewick's terms, to the third world. It is to this radical critique, which is implicit in the changing perspectives of the National Deviancy Conference (NDC) that we now turn.

The National Deviancy Conference, first suggested in the summer of

1968, was mainly the inspiration of professional sociologists receptive to the ideas of two Americans, Howard Becker and David Matza.[23] The influence of these two sociologists on the early development of the NDC is widely acknowledged, and it is only through an understanding of their work, albeit in fairly simple terms, that the student of politics can come to appreciate a radical critique of the Howard League. A useful starting point here might be to concentrate on the term deviancy, to ask why it has been preferred to the term criminal which has been used all along. The answer, in one sense, is perhaps obvious and undramatic. Deviant behaviour, to stray, as Matza puts it, from some path or pattern, is fairly widespread in our society but it is only certain forms of deviant behaviour which society chooses to criminalise. Thus, to the extent that sociologists associated with the NDC are interested in deviant behaviour in all its forms, criminal behaviour is only one aspect of this interest.

This more general concern with deviancy helps to demystify criminal behaviour. It simply becomes one aspect of a much wider social phenomenon with characteristics in common with other forms of non-criminal behaviour. It must be stressed however that no behaviour, in itself, can be deviant or criminal, it can only be so labelled as an act of social description. Smoking marijuana or fornicating in public are only deviant or criminal acts because society chooses that they should be; neither are intrinsically deviant or criminal.

For Becker and Matza the analysis so far would be unacceptable since it could easily be taken for a consensual model. By referring to 'society' choosing to label certain behaviour patterns as deviant or criminal the implication is that there is widespread and general agreement about what is to be regarded as deviant or criminal. For Becker and Matza this is clearly not the case. Their construction of social reality is a plurality of different groups, each with their own views about what should be defined as deviant or criminal. The only problem with this diversity is the relative power of these groups to translate their values into the social and legal code; some groups have demonstrably more power than others. As Becker has written: 'Differences in the ability to make rules and apply them to other people are essentially power differentials (either legal or extra legal). Those groups whose social position gives them weapons and power are best able to enforce their rules.'[24]

Becker was not intending to deny deviant or criminal behaviour or to argue that the play-off between groups could ever be equal, but he seemed to be saying in this particular context that the idea that there is a consensus which all decent people abide by is more problematic than at first appears. This emphasis on diversity, on a world of plural values, helped to give the deviant and the criminal a degree of rationality and integrity which other groups in society so often sought to deny them. Further, by stressing diversity, by pointing out that the idea of consensus was problematic, the radical pluralists entered a plea for what Jock Young has referred to as a 'culture of civility'.[25] The demand came for an end to the phoney consensus and the celebration of human diversity.

Although the radical pluralists have been widely criticised Becker is probably right to claim that he and his associates were indeed radical in that they sought to demystify the deviant and challenge the notion that those who wielded authority were safeguarding consensual norms rather than reflecting the values of a system rigged against the unorganised and the powerless.[26] To be sure, labelling theory does not tell us why people actually break the law or commit deviant acts, but then it never claimed to have an aetiological purpose. What it sought to do initially was to widen the scope of the enquiry, to look at the labellers and the labelling process as well as the labelled. In that this helped to reinstate the deviant and the criminal, to deny the commonsense assumption that such people must be, almost by definition, ill and therefore in need of treatment on the road to rehabilitation, the radical pluralists achieved a good deal. Further, by stressing as Matza did that the state through its various agencies of social control, compounds and reinforces the deviant's own sense of separateness and deviancy, a central irony in the whole process of social control was laid bare by an interactionist perspective which seemed difficult to contest.

It may come as no surprise to learn that many of the British sociologists who were sympathetic to these ideas, and more particularly those who helped to establish the NDC, had apparently been involved with left wing political groups, Anarchists, Communists and International Socialists.[27] It would, however, be inaccurate for a number of reasons to link the NDC to any of these groups, if anything *diversity* was its main characteristic. But, to the extent that commitment was mobilised, it seems to have been directed towards particular deviant groups, or organisations like Case Con (for militant social workers) and Radical Alternatives to Prison, Certainly though, there was commitment, the utilitarian values of modern industrial society were under attack from the homosexual, the dope taker and many other deviant groups in the struggle to assert the authenticity of deviancy and weaken the formal bonds of social control.

The question remains, where does the Howard League stand in relation to this reassessment of the deviant and the criminal? The answer must be that it has largely continued to work on the basis of its old assumptions. It operates a consensual model: criminals are deviants which 'society' had chosen to penalise. The role of the League is simply to ensure that the penalty imposed is not only humane, but also geared towards rehabilitation. The objective of the penal system is not just to punish the criminal but also to change him by skilled treatment into a well-adjusted and reformed person who can more easily conform to the general will. The League has remained true, in fact, to the principles it argued before the Royal Commission on the Penal System in 1965, namely, 'that the commission of an act which is prohibited by the criminal law entitles society to subject the actor to certain measures designed to reduce the probability of a repetition of the act', and the acceptance of this principle makes it possible to devise a rational penal system with the major aim of *'altering the offender's disposition* in such a way that he is unlikely to repeat his offence'.[28]

This correctional stance, so typical of the Howard League, was very much at odds with the new deviancy theory associated with the early development of the NDC. Indeed, it seemed that whereas the Howard League spoke of correctionalism and conformity other pressure groups in the penal lobby like RAP spoke of appreciation and diversity. Further, the League has traditionally been reluctant to even criticise what it took to be the consensus, to suggest that any of the criminal laws which reflected it were in any way unnecessary or undesirable. For example, in December 1944 when the 'problem' of homosexuality was raised a member of the League's Executive Committee reminded her colleagues that since it had always been the Howard League's agreed policy to accept society's definition of what constituted a criminal offence according to the law, all they could usefully do on this occasion was to discuss how best to treat homosexuals after their conviction.[29] It is true that by 1954 this hardline position had been eroded, and although the League still preferred to concentrate on treatment, it did in fact go on to recommend to the Departmental Committee on Homosexuality and Prostitution that it should no longer be an offence for males over twenty-one to have sexual relations, voluntarily and in private. More recently the League has also suggested that the term 'common prostitute' should be abolished and that neither soliciting nor kerb-crawling should in themselves be offences.[30]

To this extent, then, the Howard League is shifting its ground, it is more than ever before prepared to question what it takes to be the consensus and to argue for the decriminalising of certain offences. To deny this would be to deny the League's capacity for even limited change. On the other hand, the League's attack on the criminal law, if it can really be characterised so forcefully, is altogether less militant than RAP's critique, for the very simple reason that although the League does not agree with the whole body of criminal law, it does not have the same view of the labelling process as RAP and the radical pluralists, that is, as a process which is stacked against the unorganised and the weak and manipulated by the powerful. The League's view of social and legal reality is very different. It may have reservations but in that it does not see criminal law in such a repressive context, it holds it in far greater esteem. True, it may not be the product of a totally democratic process, but broadly speaking it represents a consensus. The League sometimes disagrees with what that consensus defines through the criminal law as punishable behaviour and in recent years has come to challenge the law on this basis; to this extent it can be said to be 'leading' public opinion. But because it accepts a consensual model this challenge is far less of a threat than RAP's radical pluralism, the inner logic of which can be interpreted as a very real threat to the stability of the existing political order.

Given that the Howard League's perspective on crime has always been influenced by academics, from Hermann Mannheim to the present Director of the Cambridge Institute of Criminology, Professor Nigel Walker, it should come as no surprise to learn that a majority of academic criminologists reinforced the League's consensual critique of the radical pluralists. After referring to the new criminologists as variously, 'young', 'blinkered' and 'political', Radzinowicz and King, for example, went on to suggest that they overestimated the heterogeneity of social values and ignored the widespread consensus, even among the oppressed, particularly when it came to condemning crimes of robbery and violence. [31] Criticism along these lines was to have an important impact on the development of the new criminology as we shall see. In the meantime though, it is worth emphasising that the Howard League welcomed criminologists like Radzinowicz and King who picked on crimes of robbery and violence. Crimes without victims might well be in a category of their own, but what about someone who robbed the local store using violence, did the new criminologists really believe that there was no consensus in society that such actions should be punished and the offender in some way treated in an effort to reform him?

These emotive examples aside, if the consensus could not be denied it had to be explained, and it was this that led many radical pluralists along the road to a Marxist analysis. For Marxists the existing legal system does not protect the interests of society as a whole, but only the interests of the ruling class. More particularly, it is through the legal system that internal order and stability is secured in order to promote the effective operation of the capitalist economy in the interests of a ruling capitalist class. However, this capitalist class does not itself rule, but controls society through the various mechanisms of the state. The state, therefore, is a coercive instrument of the capitalist class and, in that crime control is an important mechanism through which civil society is secured for the state, then criminal law is in the service of a ruling capitalist class. This analysis parts company with the position of the radical pluralists at a number of points. Most crucially, it emphasises class rather than group and locates the state as being firmly in the hands of a particular class. The state is not somehow neutral. What all this amounts to is clear. The pluralist paradigm, the vision of a society of competing groups each striving to capture the state in pursuit of their own legitimate interests, is a false vision. The crucial factor in any analysis must be class and the concomitant understanding that the state cannot simply be taken over and used in the interests of any group. Further, the vision of a plural world, of a society of competing values is simply not acceptable. When put to the test there is a clearly demonstrable consensus. But, and this is crucial, it is a consensus imposed by the hegemonic domination of the ruling capitalist class in their own interest.

It is interesting to note that as Sam Beer and colleagues had introduced American pluralism to British political scientists in the 1950s, so a decade or so later Becker and Matza were to make much the same inroads into the sociology of deviancy. But there was opposition to this later invasion and, as already indicated, it came from right across the political spectrum. For Marxists, Becker and Matza are presumably still welcome to the extent that they want to appreciate deviant behaviour, to assert its authenticity, but in other respects the debate has clearly moved on to reveal fundamental differences; a material understanding of the social process is the new point of departure. Starting with the pluralist perspective Jock Young has analysed the conflict in the following way:

> Society, they argued, did not consist of a monolithic consensus but rather a pluralistic array of values. For an action to be termed criminal or deviant demanded two activities: one, that of a group or individual acting in a particular fashion, the other, that of another group or individual with different values labelling the initial activity as deviant. Human beings acting creatively in the world constantly generated their own system of values.

> Unfortunately within the pluralistic order of society certain groups – variously and vaguely termed 'the powerful', 'the bureaucracy', 'the moral entrepreneur' – having more power than others enforced their values upon the less powerful, labelling those who infringed their rules with stereotypical tags. That is, man, who in fact, was existentially free to evolve any values he chose, or experiment with various forms of behaviour, became labelled by the authorities as in essence 'a homosexual', 'a thief', or 'a psychopath'. Moreover, this very act of labelling, by limiting the future choices of the actor and by being presented to the actor as being the truth about his nature, with all the force of authority, had a self-fulfilling effect. The old adages: 'once a thief always a thief', 'once a junkie always a junkie', became true not because, as earlier criminologists had maintained, this was the essence of the man involved but because the power of labelling transformed and cajoled men into acting and believing as if they possessed no freedom in the world.
>
> Ironically, however incisive this analysis of correctional criminology was on a preliminary level and however important its insights, the conception of human nature and social order held by these deviancy theorists was inadequate to carry the weight of their criticism. By granting men freedom in an absolute sense without acknowledging any material constraints human purpose was reduced to the level of whimsy. By characterising society as a simple diversity of values, they blinded themselves to the existence of a very real consensus – the hegemonic domination of bourgeois values. By pointing to power without analysing its class basis and the nature of the state, they transformed the actions of the powerful into an arbitrary flexing of moral muscles. In this fashion, a vulgar materialist criminology which caricatured the criminal as determined by non-purposive material factors was inverted to become an idealist criminology where crime was a product of men purposively pursuing ideas detached and free from material circumstances.[32]

This is an uncompromising statement, and in this context Becker's suggestion that it might be possible to establish a continuity between radical pluralism and Marxism is surely naive.[33] The radical pluralists are playing a very different game and as yet have developed no coherent reply to their Marxist critics who are increasingly carving out their own power base within the NDC.

To the student of politics the suggestion that criminal law is in the service of capitalism will no doubt raise some very obvious questions, not least being whether Marxists see in their own alternative reality a crime-free society. Would not Marxists agree with Durkheim that crime is a general phenomenon, that it is found not only in advanced societies but in all societies and in this sense is impossible to eradicate? Many Marxists would not agree, arguing for a commitment to socialist diversity and a set of crime-free social relations.[34] To what extent this is a plausible commitment is not really our concern, nor indeed is it our concern to develop in any detailed way the sustained and powerful critique of traditional criminology which has been undertaken by Ian Taylor, Paul Walton and Jock Young, the pacemakers in the search for a new criminology.[35] Suffice it to say that the range of their work is so massive that it will take the criminological establishment a long time to mount a counter-attack, and even then it is doubtful if it will come in any effective form from the British establishment which is so dominated by legal and psychiatric approaches to deviancy that it may not be able to generate the necessary range of expertise to attack the new criminology on its own terms.[36]

However, it is our concern to point out the fairly obvious fact that the Howard League's perspective on crime has no Marxist points of reference. Further, in as much as one of the explicit objectives of the Howard League is its aim to prevent crime, to resist attempts at breaking the criminal code, then it is clearly in the service of capitalism, an adjunct to the capitalist state. It is, therefore, no wonder that over the years the Howard League has been invited by the state to join it in the cooperative enterprise to rehabilitate the offender, to ensure that he no longer wishes to disobey the law. Of course, there have been tensions, but these have largely been a conflict between the League's progressively more liberal approach towards rehabilitation and the Home Office approach which, under pressure from conservative forces, is inclined towards simple deterrence rather than reform, punishment rather than treatment. Such are the tensions of penal reform, and even the League's sternest critics cannot deny that these tensions have sometimes been difficult to bear in purely personal terms. To listen to Lord Gardiner fending off backwoodsmen in the House of Lords, to think of the League's present chairman, Louis Blom-Cooper, making his way in the conservative world of barristers and judges, is to appreciate the hostile environment in which penal reformers operate. However, for Marxists this cannot deny what their purpose really is and that reformism is no more than the soft underbelly of the establishment.

The Howard League is unlikely to be impressed by its Marxist critics. It cannot commit itself to the large-scale dismantling of social and legal controls which, according to the relativists, would be necessary for a truly liberated society. But more than just this, it is widely accepted that the radical pluralists made a significant advance when they turned their focus on those who label and the labelling process itself. This led to a more obvious appreciation that to designate any act deviant requires two parties, the person or group behaving in a particular way, and another person or group defining that behaviour as deviant. It was one of the radical pluralists' major contentions that some groups have demonstrably more power than others to do the defining. This emphasis on the powerful, the idea that the system is somehow rigged in their favour is quite alien to the Howard League which refuses to accept that in failing to develop a critique of the labellers and the labelling process it is little more than a buttress in support of those powerful groups. On the contrary, it believes it is no more in the service of powerful groups than it is in the service of some ruling class.

Successive Home Secretaries and their civil servants have shared the League's defence, just as they share certain important assumptions about the criminal law and the penal system, and to the extent that other pressure groups in the penal lobby interpret penal policy in either a Marxist or radical pluralist context they are identified as carrying a foreign message, labelled as a potential threat to the political order and kept very firmly at the extreme edges of the policy making process. This, at least, has been the experience of Radical Alternatives to Prison.

NOTES

[1] *Bulletin of the International Penal and Penitentiary Commission,* May 1949.
[2] Quoted by J. Christoph, *Capital Punishment and British Politics,* Allen and Unwin, London, 1962, p.83.
[3] HLPR *Executive Committee Minutes,* June 1956.
[4] *Standing Committee A, Session* 1947–48, vol.1, col.971.
[5] *House of Lords Debates,* vol.231, col.464.
[6] HLPR, *Executive Committee Minutes,* November 1947.
[7] HLPR, *Annual Report,* 1947–48, p.5.
[8] The first article appeared in *The Daily Herald* on Monday 21 November 1955, p.4; the second on Tuesday 22 November 1955, p.4.
[9] *Daily Herald,* 26 November 1955, p.4.
[10] HLPR, *Executive Committee Minutes,* November 1955.

[11] HLPR, *Executive Committee Minutes,* November 1955.
[12] HLPR, *Executive Committee Minutes,* January 1956.
[13] *Penal Practice in a Changing Society,* (1959), HMSO, London, Cmnd.645, para 40.
[14] For details of this research by Dunlop and McCabe, see J.E. Hall-Williams, *The English Penal System in Transition,* Butterworth, London, 1970, pp.341–2.
[15] This conclusion, taken from Dr Grunhut's research, was actually quoted in the White Paper, *Penal Practice in a Changing Society,* para 33.
[16] One of the League's most senior academics made the point that, 'No serious research could be done without the willing cooperation of the Prison Commissioners, and that was a serious consideration and limitation.' HLPR, *Executive Committee Minutes,* June 1956. In an updated context, Stan Cohen and Laurie Taylor would be the first to agree. Their research at Durham Prison was seriously hampered by official intransigence. For what they achieved, see Stan Cohen and Laurie Taylor, *Psychological Survival,* Penguin, Harmondsworth 1972. Also note, Terence Morris, 'Some thoughts on the politics of criminology', *Times Literary Supplement,* 26 September 1975.
[17] In fairness to the League, it did become more publicly critical of detention centres during the 1960s and campaigned strongly for the closure of Moor Court. On the other hand, it is not obvious from its later memorandum on detention centres that the League had anticipated the government's intention to phase out junior detention centres as set out in the White Paper, *Children in Trouble,* (1968). See HLPR, *Annual Report,* 1967–68, pp.8–13.
[18] Martin Wright, 'Tactics of Reform' in Sean McConville (ed.), *Use of Imprisonment,* Routledge and Kegan Paul, London, 1975, p.91.
[19] M.C. Ryan, 'Radical alternatives to prison', *Political Quarterly,* vol.47, no.1, January–March 1976, pp.71–81.
[20] Notification of Annual General Meeting, circular (1975).
[21] Gordon Rose, *The Struggle for Penal Reform,* Stevens, London, 1961, pp.264–5.
[22] H. Eckstein, 'The Politics of the BMA', *Political Quarterly,* vol. 26, no.4, 1955. P. Self and H. Storing, *The State and the Farmer,* Allen and Unwin, London, 1964; M. Joel Barnett, *The Politics of Legislation,* Weidenfeld and Nicolson, London, 1969.
[23] In particular: H. Becker, *Outsiders,* Free Press, New York, 1963; D. Matza, *Delinquency and Drift,* John Wiley, New York, 1964 and D. Matza, *Becoming Deviant,* Prentice-Hall, New Jersey, 1969.

The logic of the formation of the NDC as such, as an alternative forum to the Cambridge Institute of Criminology and the Home Office

Research Unit, has been clearly set out by Paul Wiles in his introduction to *The Sociology of Crime and Delinquency in Britain*, vol.2, *The New Criminologies*, Martin Robertson, London, 1976.
[24] H. Becker, *Outsiders*, Free Press, New York, 1963, pp.17–18.
[25] Ian Taylor, Paul Walton and Jock Young (eds), *Critical Criminology*, Routledge and Kegan Paul, London, 1975. See essay by Jock Young, 'Working class criminology', p.66.
[26] P. Rock and M. McIntosh, *Deviance and Social Control*, Tavistock Publications, London, 1974. See essay by H. Becker, 'Labelling theory reconsidered', p.62.
[27] See essay by Stan Cohen, 'Criminology and the sociology of deviance in Britain', in P. Rock and M. McIntosh, *Deviance and Social Control*, Tavistock Publications, London, 1974, p.27.
[28] Minutes of evidence taken before the *Royal Commission on the Penal System in England and Wales*, HMSO, 1967, pp.143–4.
[29] HLPR, *Executive Committee Minutes*, December 1944.
[30] HLPR, *Newsletter*, no.14, May 1975, p.2.
[31] *Times Literary Supplement*, 26 September 1975, pp.1088–9.
[32] See Jock Young's introduction to Frank Pearce's *Crimes of the Powerful*, Pluto Press, London, 1976, pp.12–13.
[33] Discussed by Frank Pearce, *Crimes of the Powerful*, Pluto Press, London, 1976, p.45.
[34] This is not a commonly accepted view. See the debate between Ian Taylor and Paul Walton and Paul Hirst in *Critical Criminology*, Routledge and Kegan Paul, London, 1975, pp.203ff.
[35] Ian Taylor, Paul Walton and Jock Young, *The New Criminology*, Routledge and Kegan Paul, London, 1973.
[36] Indeed, the British establishment seems determined to ignore the new criminology and the sharp edge of the debate, where it exists, is between Ian Taylor and colleagues and Althuserian Marxists like Paul Hirst who assert that a Marxist criminology is not possible. For an interesting comment on this debate see Colin Sumner, 'Marxism and deviancy theory', in Paul Wiles (ed.), *The Sociology of Crime and Delinquency in Britain*, vol.2, *The New Criminologies*, Martin Robertson, London, 1976.

5 Radical Alternatives to Prison

Although the Howard League had little faith in the staying power of the Prison Medical Reform Council, Gordon Rose is wrong to suggest that the Council soon faded away altogether.[1] True, its activities were temporarily suspended with the passing of the Criminal Justice Act in 1948, but by the early 1950s it was back in business and survived in one form or another long enough to attract some new recruits from the Campaign for Nuclear Disarmament and more particularly the Committee of 100. Exactly what the Council did to improve the lot of the imprisoned nuclear disarmers is not easy to determine. Probably its pressure achieved very little by way of specific reforms. Much more likely is that its critical presence helped to guarantee militant disarmers better treatment from the prison authorities, than otherwise might have been the case. That this was a credible role is obvious enough and certainly it contributed something towards making the Council's presence in the penal lobby more visible. On the other hand, it was not sufficient in itself to attract a large following and by 1965 the Council's membership was only around 100. It was from this relatively weak base that the Council submitted evidence to the Royal Commission on the Penal System.[2]

It must be admitted that the Council's oral evidence was muddled and at times even contradictory. If the published exchanges were in any way typical of how Royal Commissions conduct their business then it would be difficult not to agree with Professor Radzinowicz who argues that their methods of investigation are no longer appropriate. However, the Council's position as a reformist pressure group was easily identifiable. None of its representatives spoke in favour of abolishing prisons altogether. Their main concerns were much more limited, namely, better prison conditions, a more sensible method of classifying offenders, greater emphasis on rehabilitation rather than on deterrence and so on. All very predictable. The only way in which the Council really showed itself to be out of step with other reform groups in the penal lobby was its willingness to expose the brutality and corruption of the prison system, to argue that prisoners were beaten-up by warders, to suggest that prison medical reports were not all that they should be. This frankness was more than welcome. Far too many groups in the penal lobby, groups who knew well enough about the dark side of prison life, were prepared to remain obsequious rather than risk being labelled 'irresponsible'. This difference aside, the Council had much the same objectives as other reform groups like the Howard League and its continual independent existence in less militant times must have always been in doubt. Thus, with the decline of CND and the activities of the Committee of 100 the Council was, by 1970, all but moribund. It was in October 1970 that the Council was effectively outflanked by a ginger group, later to become Radical Alternatives to Prison, which had been the inspiration of the late Sandra Roszkowski and Ros Kane.

A provisional manifesto signed by Roskowski and Kane was circulated to members of the ginger group which met just before what was to be the Prison Reform Council's last AGM. [3] The manifesto was very general and at that time contained no overwhelming commitment to alternatives, but as soon as this commitment began to emerge it became even more obvious that the once radical Prison Reform Council would have to go in favour of RAP. The demand for alternatives rather than reform was the only way forward. The Council was subsequently dissolved and its slender assets transferred to RAP. [4]

Canon Collins was closely identified with the Campaign for Nuclear Disarmament. It was therefore not surprising that Christian Action, an organisation founded by Collins after the last war, had taken a special interest in the activities of the Prison Reform Council, In the context of its dissolution, a member of the ginger group circulated by Roszkowski and Kane was Colin Hodgetts, then Christian Action's full time Director. Hodgetts gave practical support to RAP from the very beginning, offering its activists office space in the early days and then in May 1971 inviting them to register RAP as a third project with Christian Action. This was a generous invitation since it included a salary for one full time worker and a separate allowance to cover telephone charges and stationery. The trial went reasonably well and by January 1972 RAP agreed to increase its financial dependency on Christian Action by registering as a full project, though this decision was not taken without some argument. [5] In the first place many of RAP's members were anything but christian and they were not at all happy to be associated with the Church of England, even if it meant following a maverick like Canon Collins. It was then, as Fenner Brockway had earlier written to say, a question of balancing an increase in technical efficiency against the taint of Christianity. [6] Brockway was inclined to be pragmatic, and no doubt if this had been all that was at stake most of RAP's supporters would have been equally pragmatic. After all, how could they match Christian Action's new and increased offer of two full time salaries and a permanent office? [7] But clearly there was more to it than this. In particular, what would happen if RAP's policy at any point differed from that of Christian Action, would RAP be expected to modify its views? Colin Hodgetts was not unaware of the possibility that there might be disagreements, and that they might conceivably be serious enough to force RAP out of Christian Action altogether. However, this was the worst that could happen. Given the spirit of cooperation, Hodgetts felt confident that such a situation would never arise. A skilfully worded memorandum from Christian Action was to sum up the problem:

> If Christian Action feels that a policy or action pursued by RAP or a statement issued by it is widely divergent from Christian Action's own social ideals, the matter will be raised in the first instance with the full time worker and if necessary taken further to a meeting of RAP activists or in the final resort to a general meeting of RAP members. This will not be interpreted so as to interfere in any way with the work, policies or statements of RAP, but equally it is inevitable that repeated failure to agree on major issues will lead to a cessation of the present relationship between RAP and Christian Action. In the light of RAP's policy and achievements to date, there is no reason to foresee such a breach in what has been an arrangement of mutual trust and respect. [8]

This apparently sensitive but realistic approach persuaded RAP that Christian Action's continued sponsorship would be a good thing. It is clear though that some of the more politically aware activists were uneasy, believing that Christian Action's commitment to fundamental social and economic change was no longer as strong as it had been, if indeed it had ever really been very strong at all. This political assessment of Christian Action was crucial since a major contention in RAP's provisional manifesto had been that most crimes are the reflection of an unequal profit-minded society which had to be radically restructured. [9] To what extent Christian Action would baulk at RAP's radicalism was thus an important question, but one which had to wait for an answer in practice.

Christian Action's increased support for RAP came at a good time since it was during the first half of 1972 that the campaign to halt the rebuilding of Holloway prison was reaching its climax. Arguably this was one of RAP's most impressive campaigns and it is worth considering in some detail. RAP's interest in the problem of women in prison was given a public platform as early as May 1971 when a one day conference on 'Women in Prison and the Alternatives' was organised at Kingsway Hall. A long list of well known speakers was invited and RAP was pleased with the turn-out of around 200. It was this meeting which encouraged RAP to organise a systematic campaign against the rebuilding of Holloway and by the end of May a committee for that purpose had already met and drawn up a comprehensive strategy.

In December 1968, James Callaghan, then Home Secretary, announced the government's long term strategy to deal with what he referred to as the 'female penal problem'. Callaghan's basic strategy was to divide the existing penal institutions for women and girls into two groups, one designed to serve the north, the other the south. Ideally, each would have a comprehensive range of institutions: a closed prison, a remand centre, closed borstal facilities and so on. Holloway was to be the remand centre for the south east and the closed prison for the south. It was also to provide certain country wide facilities, including psychiatric and medical services. Further, in recognition of the belief that most women and girls in custody require psychiatric and medical treatment, Mr Callaghan announced that Holloway would be redeveloped on its existing site as what amounted to a secure hospital where custodial facilities would be minimal.[10]

Organising the redevelopment of Holloway was entrusted in the early stages to the Holloway Project Group, made up of representatives from the Prison Department and the Department of Health and Social Security.[11] The main purpose of the Project Group seems to have been to ensure that the new regime's underlying principles were very firmly established before the design team got down to any detailed planning. The Group came up with a treatment regime based on three themes, the first being 'immediate help', including perhaps medical treatment if required, and almost certainly welfare help to advise the prisoner about her personal affairs such as the problem of finding someone to look after her children. Second, there would be long term medical and psychiatric help, perhaps a planned programme of group therapy. Finally a very real effort was to be made to create a vital community in which human relationships could be formed so that women could learn to cope with one another in a way that would help them to lead more settled lives when they returned to the community outside.[12]

It was progress on this thoroughly planned 'secure hospital' with its wide range of treatments to be administered by a highly trained staff that RAP's campaign committee set out to halt.[13] [14] At first it seemed that public support might be difficult to enlist since the Home

Office had worked very hard to present the new building as a 'secure hospital' and a place where prisoners would be pleased to stay, rather than a prison. But the Project Group could not go on using manipulative language like 'the impression of normality' and 'the appearance of freedom' without revealing the real purpose of the new Holloway.[15] Katrin Fitzherbert's *New Society* article on Holloway, which was more like a piece from the *Architect's Journal* than a serious contribution on women in prison, made the point that if the new Holloway was ever finished it would be a study in ambiguity.[16]

The most pressing aspect of the whole business for RAP's campaign committee was the certain knowledge that staff training was under way and work on demolishing the old buildings already started. A short, sharp campaign was therefore necessary, but exactly how this could be mobilised was in some doubt, particularly given the committee's early decision to make their case against the new Holloway a well researched one. What emerged was a mixture of exhibitions and demonstrations in the short term, culminating in the issue of a detailed and comprehensive pamphlet in May 1972, *Alternatives to Holloway.* The short term strategy was quite successful, but it could not compare with the attention focussed on Holloway as a result of imprisoning the unfortunate Pauline Jones.

Pauline Jones was jilted by her boyfriend, suffered a miscarriage and then, in a deep post-natal depression, snatched a baby, a crime for which she was imprisoned for three years. Committed to Holloway prison she reacted by cutting her wrists and taking an overdose. RAP's view of the sentence, even when it was subsequently reduced on appeal to twenty-one months, was that it was totally unjustified and, moreover, in danger of making a woman whose problems were basically temporary, into a permanent social 'inadequate'.[17] Imprisoning Pauline Jones in Holloway would achieve nothing, it only symbolised the bankrupt nature of the penal system. It was in this critical spirit that RAP members joined in the demonstration against her imprisonment which was held outside Holloway on 16 January 1972. There was a good turn out with the media appearing in force and on the surface the demonstrators should have been satisfied. RAP, however, although deeply concerned about the plight of Pauline Jones, also felt that the demonstration should be used to point out that prisons in general were irrelevant and destructive. To the extent that only *Time Out* made this point the demonstration was only a qualified success.[18]

By the spring of 1972 RAP's pamphlet, *Alternatives to Holloway,* was nearing completion and preparations were put in hand to organise a series of activities to more or less coincide with its publication. After a brief but pointed introduction the pamphlet concentrated on the facts of female crime in general, arguing that it is relatively rare and for the most part petty and that indictable or more serious offences are rarer among females than males.[19] Having considered the extent and seriousness of female crime, *Alternatives to Holloway* then turned its attention to the very small percentage of women who are actually held in custody, arguing that too many females were being remanded in custody unnecessarily and a large number of prison sentences were for offences which would be better dealt with in other ways.[20] But what of Holloway in particular, that after all was the pamphlet's principal target?

The Holloway facts were based mainly on sample data. A high number of receptions were concerned with property offences (mainly shop-lifting) and, predictably, non-indictable offences associated with drunkenness, drugs and prostitution. Further, Holloway receives a higher proportion of remands than other women's prisons and of the 2500–2700 or so females received each year into Holloway, three-quarters of them have yet to be sentenced, and when they are, less than 20 per cent are subsequently sent to prison.[21] What RAP felt to be true about women in prison was also true about Holloway in particular: it contained too many women on remand who need not be there and a number of unnecessarily sentenced

> women and girls with a considerable mixture of personal and social problems, among which crime is but one minor aspect. Hardly any of the offences could in any way be considered a menace – a slight nuisance perhaps, but of no real consequence to the social order, and certainly not requiring the sledgehammer of prison.[22]

Having considered the problem *Alternatives to Holloway* then went on to offer some solutions. First, there was the question of remands in custody. There was little doubt in RAP's mind that the amendments to the Magistrates Courts Act (1952) made by the Criminal Justice Act (1967) in respect of remands in custody for reports after conviction but before sentence, and remands for reports before conviction when the court is convinced that the accused did the act, should be repealed. To limit remands in both these cases and, indeed, to limit the use of remands before trial, a simple presumption was needed in favour of bail as a right, the onus being on the authorities to establish that the defendant was incapable of exercising that right according to a system of checks similar to those devised in the Manhatten Bail Project.[23]

Second, and separate from the problem of remands in custody, the pamphlet turned its detailed attention on those convicted women who were incarcerated in Holloway. RAP's position was quite straightforward: a whole range of offences, from those involving alcoholism and drug addiction to child cruelty and petty theft, should not result in offenders being sent to Holloway, indeed, in many cases they should not be prosecuted at all. On alcoholism, for example, RAP could see no point in fining people for offences associated with drunkenness and then when they could not pay the fine sending them to prison. Attention was drawn to a detailed study of Holloway between 1964–67 in which sixteen female 'drunkenness offenders' apparently accounted for an average of 100 annual receptions, which was then 10 per cent of Holloway's intake of women under sentence. One unfortunate woman had twenty-four receptions in Holloway in a single year. Most of the offenders in this category are widowed, single or homeless.[24] For RAP there was no point in sending them to Holloway but an alternative strategy was urgently required.

The main thrust of RAP's strategy was the idea of progression. Women alcoholics should at first be directed to reception centres which would provide not only medical facilities but act as referral agencies directing alcoholics to temporary shelters located where they tend to congregate, at large railway stations for example. From there they should be referred to long stay centres like those run by the Simon Community deliberately organised to cope with a range of clients from women who may need more or less permanent help to those whose needs are more periodic. One of the sad truths about RAP's alternative for women alcoholics was its realism, its recognition that the idea of progression in no way denied that for many women there is no 'cure'; they have been so physically and psychologically battered that the best society can do is to provide them with basic support and comfort until they die.[25]

What RAP's campaign committee did for alcoholics it also did for other groups such as drug addicts, prostitutes and those who maltreat babies. In *Alternatives to Holloway* it suggested a whole range of community-based projects to make prison for women seem irrelevant. The new Holloway was a £6½ million folly which would still receive women unnecessarily labelled as 'criminal' and then 'treat' them in an institutional setting which was almost certain to fail. In some quarters their crushing indictment was well received. Jill Tweedie in *The Guardian*, for example, referred to *Alternatives to Holloway* as making out an 'excellent case' against imprisoning women and gave full details of RAP's rally at the Central Hall, Westminster (6 June 1972) which was to be the climax of the Holloway Campaign.[26]

RAP would be the first to admit that the rally was a failure. To start with, the Central Hall, Westminster was far too large for the sort of gathering RAP could muster. Second, the speakers invited were not all strictly in line with RAP's policy and this created a mixture of confusion and resentment. Third, as the rally was held too long after the publication of *Alternatives to Holloway*, the impact of a good press was dissipated. All these factors, combined with technical problems, produced a fairly dull event which many MPs left early to return to the Commons. What was to have been the climax of RAP's campaign, then, turned out to be quite the opposite, an anti-climax. [27] But what of the overall campaign? How successful was RAP's attempt to stop the rebuilding of Holloway?

At one level the answer is obvious enough, the campaign failed and Holloway was rebuilt. To explain this by referring to a combination of tactical errors, would clearly be wrong. Much more crucial was that the objective itself was never really possible. Edward Heath's Conservative Government had taken over Labour's commitment to rebuild the old Holloway and by 1971 a start had already been made. There was never any real possibility that the government would turn back at so late a stage, that is, to admit in public that its policy on female offenders was totally misconceived, even if it thought that RAP was right. Failure to realise this was not only sad for the false hopes it held out to Holloway's 'regulars', it was also a blow to RAP's morale, and one of the campaign's organisers was quick to imply that RAP, like any other pressure group, could not be expected to sustain one hopeless campaign after another; future objectives would have to be well within RAP's capacity.[28] On the plus side, there is very little doubt that the campaign made the problem of women in prison more visible than it had been in the past and in doing so made RAP itself more visible. As a relatively new pressure group in the penal lobby it gained valuable publicity from the campaign. The loss of morale needs to be set against the very real gain of a definite focus on which RAP's members could build a more active involvement.

It is possible to argue that other groups played a part in raising the problems of women in prison. In 1972, for example, the Howard League's pamphlet on *Granting Bail in Magistrates' Courts* used some of the research material which RAP had relied on for *Alternatives to Holloway*. All the same, the pamphlet in question was exactly what it claimed to be, a tough-minded demonstration of how bail is denied to defendents of both sexes when it could, in fact, be safely granted; it never intended to place special emphasis on the position of women on remand in custody and by definition, it did not set out to raise a whole range of other fundamental questions about women in prison;

that was left to RAP. Further, the way in which these fundamental questions were raised by RAP was in sharp contrast to the way the Howard League conducted its business. At one level, of course, the difference was obvious; RAP demonstrated, and was hostile to the bureaucracy, displaying the sort of bad manners which the League thought intolerable and counter-productive. But the difference went deeper than just style. RAP's campaign against the new Holloway was conducted within the framework of a radical critique, part radical pluralist, part implied Marxist, which was altogether too much for the Howard League. In a letter from the Holloway campaign committee in February 1972 considerable stress was placed upon the idea that the campaign was not only to be interpreted widely in the sense that it was about the role of women in society in general,[29] but that, more crucially, it was about 'the social inequalities of opportunity and of power' that exist to determine exactly what should be regarded as criminal, and how these inequalities discriminate against the disadvantaged and the poor in favour of the powerful and the wealthy. As *Alternatives to Holloway* was to put it:

> Underlying the plans for a new Holloway (and for other new and bigger prisons), is the unquestioned acceptance of the whole superstructure of the law, the courts, the police, the definitions of who is 'criminal', in a word, of 'Justice'. The whole process of labelling a person as a 'criminal', of which prison is a small but important part, is taken for granted. It is very important to see that the definition of certain sorts of acquisitiveness and violence as 'criminal' and the acceptance of other sorts of acquisitiveness and violence as commendable, reflects and perpetuates the vested interests and inequalities of power, wealth and status that have characterised British society from the time of the despotic barons, through powerful landowners and ruthless industrialists to today. The law, its substance and its application, are rooted in the inequalities of the past. Thus the law has been compared to a cobweb – it lets the big bumble bee through and catches only small insects.[30]

To speak of 'curing criminality' in this context is simply official obfuscation, a deceit practised on behalf of the powerful.

Even if the Howard League had reservations about the new Holloway, even if it could be shown that the League had argued for the decriminalisation of those offences which helped to fill Holloway to the brim, its critique of the penal system had well defined limits which RAP's analysis went rudely beyond, attacking as it did the

the powerful and the wealthy. This was difficult for the League's members to get into focus. The old Prison Reform Council had often accused the Howard League of not shouting loudly enough, but RAP seemed to want the League to shout a different message altogether. For the penal lobby this new political message was difficult to cope with, it was somehow hard to understand what politics had to do with penal reform. This genuine conceptual difficulty, which illustrates how successful official obfuscation has been over the years, was vividly demonstrated by an anonymous correspondent in the *Prison Service Journal.* The contributor had once considered himself a radical, but after attending RAP's rally on Holloway at the Central Hall he realised more than ever that he was 'decidedly square'. He reflected on his reaction: could it have been the way the rally was presented, or was he perhaps annoyed because RAP's members were amateurs, and not professionally involved with the day to day problems of coping with those who have broken the law? No, he thought that there was more to it than that:

> I came away with the slight but unmistakeable sense of exploitation, that people's goodwill and integrity is being used for other purposes besides that of penal reform. I believe profoundly that crime and punishment must be kept out of the political arena. It is far too emotive and emotional an area to allow it to be used for political ends.[31]

The poverty of this man's vision was matched by others in the penal lobby, others perhaps who knew better than he did exactly what was at stake.

The collapse of the Holloway campaign did not mean that RAP stopped taking a close interest in the question of women and crime. In June 1973, for example, the newsletter carried a very critical review of the ISTD's conference on 'Women Offenders'. The governor of Styal Women's Prison was taken to task for trying to 'sell' the new Holloway and the conference generally was characterised as being devoid of ideas and geared to serving the establishment.[32] RAP was equally hostile to what the establishment had to say about prostitution in its 1974 working party on vagrancy and street offences. The main problem for RAP in this context was that the Home Office working party followed recommendations which had earlier been made by the Wolfenden Committee in 1957. Briefly, the Committee had argued that while prostitution should not in itself be regarded as a criminal offence, the law should provide that the streets were clear of importuning prostitutes who might cause offence to the ordinary citizen, and to this end it was recommended that to loiter or solicit in a public place should be an offence. This was later incorporated into the Street Offences Act 1959. Members of the 1974 working party felt that this Act, based as they saw it on sound principles, was working well and required very little alteration.[33] RAP took a very different view, arguing that although the Street Offences Act 1959 had been successful to the extent that it had all but eliminated soliciting in public places, it discriminated against women by fining or imprisoning only the prostitute and not her client. But beyond this, RAP's position was that soliciting should cease to be a criminal offence and the public, if need be, should be prepared to put up with the inconvenience.[34]

There were also other aspects of the working party's agreement with Wolfenden which made RAP unhappy, not least being its almost casual acceptance of imprisonment as the ultimate sanction against soliciting. The working party pointed out that Wolfenden had recommended progressively heavier fines for soliciting, and where monetary penalties had failed to deter, imprisonment. This tough line was endorsed by the working party on the basis that previous legislation without the sanction of imprisonment had 'failed to keep the streets clear'. No pretence was made that a spell inside Holloway or any other custodial establishment would have a rehabilitative impact, deterrence was the only motive. Needless to say RAP also endorsed those other groups in the penal lobby who pointed out that the prostitute had more than a good chance of being fined or imprisoned because she appeared in the court charged as a 'common prostitute', that is, already labelled in such a way that her alleged offence seemed highly probable. The idea that the label 'common prostitute' might be done away with was rejected by the working party on the basis that it would make the job of establishing guilt more difficult and therefore commit more police manpower to clearing the streets than the service could possibly afford! Given this attitude it is not surprising that the suggestion that the police should have to rely on the evidence of the solicited person was ruled out as a 'non-starter'.

It might be argued in the working party's defence against the charge of total complacency that it did at least depart from the Wolfenden recommendations in one important respect, namely, that it sought to criminalise males who solicited by kerb-crawling. This gesture towards equality was not much appreciated by RAP since it was pointed out that kerb-crawling, as the working party saw it, would be far more difficult to prove than female soliciting.[35] This bias was not surprising since the idea that prostitution might be a reflection of the role of women as sex objects in a male-dominated society would hardly occur to a Home Office working party of twelve men and one woman so why expect any new proposals to differ in their pattern of discrimination from those in the past?

RAP's comments on the Working Party on Vagrancy and Street Offences Working Paper were submitted in March 1975 and this prompted the suggestion that a Women and Crime group should be formed to consider not only prostitution but also offences such as rape and wife battering. This suggestion was readily accepted and by November 1972 six meetings had been held in the Polytechnic of Central London.[36] Interest in women and crime during this period (and during the early months of 1976) was heightened by two events. First, there was the formation of a pressure group for prostitutes, PUSSI, Prostitutes United for Social and Sexual Integration.[37] This caused a lot of public comment, not least that its 'appalling title' tended to trivialise its serious purpose. However, Helen Buckingham who formed the group made out a credible case for its existence and RAP's Women and Crime group soon offered its support. Second, and perhaps less dramatic than PUSSI, was a series of articles on women in prison which appeared in the *Yorkshire Post.* These articles led to a spate of questions in Parliament about the use of drugs in women's prisons, about post and ante-natal care and the policy of allowing children to remain in prison with their mothers.[38] In one form or another, then, questions about women and crime were in the public conscience during the winter of 1975–76. This is of some significance because it was during the early part of this winter that RAP's Women and Crime group requested permission to visit Holloway to see just how much had really changed. RAP waited for an answer from the Governor, not for weeks but for months. Eventually a reply was received dated 18 June 1976, it read:

> I have today received a reply from headquarters regarding the visit to Holloway which you requested. After careful consideration it has been decided that your request must be refused, as it is not normally departmental policy to admit groups of people from unofficial organisations to view Prison Department establishments.

The most interesting facet of this reply from the Governor was not so much its refusal, but the terms of that refusal. If RAP was an 'unofficial organisation' and therefore unable to visit Holloway, what was an official organisation, and what precisely did headquarters regard as official? Was it perhaps the Red Cross and the WRVS, groups which actually carry on voluntary work at Holloway and other penal establishments? Was the position taken up by headquarters that access should be granted to voluntary groups as such, but not pressure groups? The simple answer to all these questions is that headquarters defines organisations as official or unofficial on the basis of whether or not they are radical and troublesome. If they are radical and troublesome they are kept at arm's length, if not, they are accepted, even to the extent of being allowed inside custodial institutions like Holloway. The distinction between voluntary groups and pressure groups is of little significance. The straightforward political nature of this particular labelling process was clearly revealed in November 1976 when in reply to a written question from Robert Bean, Labour MP for Rochester and Chatham, the Secretary of State for the Home Department made it clear that although RAP's request to visit Holloway had been turned down the Howard League had made a similar request and this had been granted.[39] In other words, it would have been surprising if the League's request had not been granted since its status as Her Majesty's Opposition on Prisons implies that while it might indeed criticise the Prison Department it is loyal, and thus officially recognised, to the extent that it does not challenge the legitimacy of the prison system. RAP on the other hand is very much an unofficial opposition since it demands an alternative to the existing prison system and as such refuses to acknowledge its legitimacy.

RAP's continuing focus on Holloway and, more particularly, its early attempt to stop its rebuilding was to form the basis of a much wider campaign to turn the government away from its planned programme of prison building, a programme which in RAP's early days seemed to be geared to a massive expansion. For example, no sooner had the Holloway campaign got underway in the spring of 1971 when it was forecast in July that more than twenty new custodial establishments were needed in the southeast of England alone. The existing prisons, borstals and so on, could take about 13,000 inmates, but by the late 1970s an additional 7,000 places would be needed, about half for adults and half for young offenders. True, these figures for the southeast were modified in 1973 but even then 6,000 new places were planned for, an expansion which was based on an estimate from the Home Office that there would be between 55,000 and 60,000 people in prison in the country as a whole during the 1980s. Faced with this sort of projection RAP set about a short, sharp campaign against the prison building programme by circulating those of its members who lived near to the new prison (or prison expansion) sites suggesting that they campaign locally. A brief specimen letter was enclosed already addressed to one of the local newspapers. There was no pressure on members to accept this letter as it stood. On the contrary, a good deal of additional information, factual and comparative, was included so that members could prepare a more thorough letter if they felt so inclined. This strategy had the great advantage of involving provincial members in a campaign run by London RAP, a gesture which as things turned out was to be of little consequence. The reason for this was in some ways a pleasant embarrassment, namely that the launching of RAP's campaign in December 1973 coincided with the announcement by Chancellor Anthony Barber of public expenditure cuts which put a stop to any fresh starts on new prison buildings. This announcement was welcomed by RAP, but clearly it did not represent a firm commitment by the government to alternatives and the danger here was that in the absence of such a firm commitment a restricted building programme might lead in the future to a grossly overcrowded prison system which would erupt with even more violence than it had done in 1972. This is not to suggest that there was no government commitment to encouraging alternatives. There was, and *New Society* was correct to suggest that the government's expenditure patterns reflected this change.[40] However, the question was whether the new emphasis, given the latest round of cuts in the prison building programme, was anything like sufficient to avoid more overcrowding.

The prison riots of 1972 were important for RAP in several ways, and not least because they helped to launch a prisoners union, PROP (Preservation of the Rights of Prisoners). Originally formed by two ex-prisoners Doug Curtis and Dick Pooley in May 1972 PROP gained massive public attention in August of the same year after its coordination of a nationwide gaol demonstration. The magnitude of this demonstration by prisoners was not denied even by the Home Office which is normally tight-lipped about such matters. Indeed, with demonstrating prisoners on the rooftops waving PROP banners there was little point in trying to play down the intensity of what was happening. Indeed, thanks mainly to PROP's agitation the Home Secretary Robert Carr was later to refer to 1972 as a turbulent and difficult year in which there had been no fewer than 130 demonstrations affecting 41 different establishments.

As Laurie Taylor has suggested, it was perhaps inevitable that PROP's rapid rise to national prominence, the attention it received from the media and so on, was all too much for a group whose organisation from the start was sketchy.[41] PROP's quick decision to decentralise after the demonstrations in August 1972, for example, seems to have been partly in response to the tensions of not having an organisational structure strong enough to make national policy statements in any way meaningful. In this sense to talk of the group's 'subsequent decline' can imply more than is either fair or accurate. No one would deny that it lost considerable momentum after the heady days of 1972. However, during the last year or two the activities of London PROP (organised by Ted Ward) have received a sympathetic and consistent national press.

The list of demands put forward by PROP over the years has usually been characterised by a view of the prisoners' movement which transcends traditional 'bread and butter' issues, the right, as it were, to better pay and conditions. Such demands have of course been included but PROP has been more concerned to democratise and prise open the prison system, to win for prisoners the right to vote in local and national elections, to elect and appoint representatives of PROP to negotiate with prison staff and the Home Office itself, to guarantee unfettered access to outside legal advice, to receive uncensored mail and to be legally represented at internal disciplinary hearings; it is for rights like these that PROP has been campaigning. What, then, has been RAP's reaction to PROP?

Right from the start RAP welcomed PROP's formation, but at the same time drew a distinction between its own policies and those which it understood PROP to be following. RAP's newsletter outlines the differences in the context of an article by Terence Morris comparing both groups:

> Morris . . . failed to realise that RAP and PROP have very different aims and ideas. This confusion seems widespread. PROP has much more short term reformist goals, with the improvement of the prisoner's lot as its chief objective. Abolition and alternatives to prison are often thrown in as an after-thought, but many of their members seem to believe that prisons are an inevitable part of the social system. RAP's aim is the total abolition of the prison structure. The short term objectives are concentration on experiments on long range alternatives to social deviancy. The alternatives would be based on much greater community participation and would also encompass radical changes in the society that creates such deviancy. The after-thought with RAP is the immediate – the brutalisation, the humiliations suffered by individuals. Both approaches are important and neither organisation can cover both.[42]

This statement deserves careful consideration both for what it says and what it implies. In the first place, it stresses that PROP wished to concentrate on improving the prisoner's lot whereas RAP sought to emphasise alternatives. This is fair and obvious enough. The difficulty comes though with the implication that it is only by RAP's emphasis on alternatives that progress towards abolition can be achieved and that however laudable PROP's reformist efforts might be to improve the prisoner's lot they are no part of a strategy for abolition. In other words, there is no continuum between prison reform and prison abolition. This analysis had fateful consequences since it meant that at best, that is, even if RAP came to believe that PROP was genuinely and firmly committed to abolition, there could be nothing more than a modest cooperation between the two groups because PROP's efforts were not thought of as being connected in any way with RAP's over-riding concern, abolition. It was just this that lay behind RAP's tepid response to Ted Ward's suggestion that RAP and PROP should think of 'pooling their resources and working more closely in the future.'[43] The validity of RAP's position in this context will be considered later. In the meantime, it is of interest that even allowing for any differences that there might have been between RAP and PROP the Home Office was inclined in the early days at least to tar both groups with the same radical and disruptive brush and when it realised that their representatives were to attend a conference presided over by Lords Kilbrandon and Gardiner in November 1972 it advised its own staff and the Prison Officers Association not to attend.

Because RAP does not wish to concentrate on improving the prisoner's lot should not be taken to mean that it has no close interest in what happens in prisons, nor indeed that it has made no efforts to contact the imprisoned. The difficulty here is trying to find a way round the Official Secrets Act. What really happens on the inside is shrouded in secrecy and even a simple thing like getting letters to interested prisoners is by no means easy. What happens to RAP literature can vary. It can simply disappear, or more usually, it is placed in 'the prisoner's property', and is therefore only available to him on release. If RAP writes to enquire why its literature is being withheld the most popular reason given is that prisoners are not normally allowed to correspond with (or be visited by) persons who were unknown to them prior to their reception into custody. It is clear in such cases that the word normally is being used to discriminate against radical groups like RAP. The fact that some Governors are less hostile than this and allow prisoners to have access to RAP literature only serves to demonstrate the arbitrary nature of the whole censorship system.

Given RAP's wish to concentrate on alternatives it was not surprising that it had much to say about government experiments in this field and, in particular, the operation of Community Service Orders. The idea of Community Service Orders originated with the Wootton Report, published in 1970[44], which proposed that instead of imprisonment there should be, in appropriate cases, an alternative sentence involving part time work which was of real benefit or service to the community. (The exact amount of time which offenders would spend on such part time work would be determined by the Courts, but in any event it should not be more than 120 hours.) The Report was optimistic that its 'most ambitious proposal' would be accepted by the government because it appealed to so many interests in the penal lobby.[45] For those with economy in mind part time work in service to the community was obviously cheaper than imprisonment; for others it could be seen as embodying an important moral principle, the reparation by offenders to the community; for others still it would have the advantage of bringing the offender into close touch with those in the community who most urgently need help and support. This last point is crucial since it implies Wootton's rehabilitative ideal, the notion that by being involved with those who most urgently need help and support the offender will somehow become a better person, more sanguine about his own future, more balanced and responsible in his outlook on society. This process of adjustment would be encouraged if it could be arranged for the offender to carry out his tasks under the 'wholesome influence' of those people who voluntarily give up their time to help the underprivileged.[46]

It is important to point out that although the Wootton Report intended part time work in the community to be used very definitely as an alternative to imprisonment, it was not exclusively for that purpose, but could be used as an alternative to a fine or in cases where the Court felt something was needed to stiffen probation. This meant that courts were to be given an alternative sentence which could be so widely used as to make the provision and organisation of part time community work a major administrative challenge. Wootton acknowledged this challenge and set out very clearly the conditions necessary for the success of its proposal. First, there was the need to ensure that the supply of part time community work was sufficient and suitable. Second, Wootton was aware that a link was required between those voluntary organisations providing part time community work and the Courts, an organisation geared to interviewing offenders, assessing their potential and then placing them with the appropriate voluntary organisation. After consultation it was decided that the best people to staff such an organisation would be probation officers. To some extent this was a logical choice. In the first place it had been argued that community service would only work if ordered selectively. An important element in the selection process would be the probation officer's social enquiry report which the court would have to consider before deciding whether or not to order part time work in the community. Thus, the probation service being involved right from the start, to transfer the organisation to another group of professionals would be pointless, particularly given the probation officer's role as a servant to the court which placed him in an ideal position to 'report back' if the offender was felt to be slacking on the job. That this would place an increased burden on the probation service was obvious enough and Wootton argued that it would need to be strengthened, particularly on the administrative side and special training might be necessary in certain cases. Finally, and on a cautious note, the Report agreed that its proposal for community service contained many practical difficulties and because of this a few pilot schemes should be tried, closely monitored by an appropriately designed research project to test their effectiveness.[47]

In an attempt to get a clearer picture of just what those difficulties were and what arrangements would be best to overcome them, the government set up a Working Group on Community Service by Offenders. The Working Group began by testing one of the Wootton Report's major assumptions, namely, that there was, in fact, sufficient part time community work available. The replies received by the Group indicated that this assumption had been a correct one for work was certainly available and would fall into two broad categories: first, work of a practical nature not involving personal relationships with clients, cleaning rubbish tips, helping with reclamation schemes and so on, and second, tasks which did involve personal relationships with clients, say acting as a driver for the elderly or the disabled. Some doubts were expressed by local authorities about whether or not they would be prepared to allow offenders to enter into personal relationships with those directly in their charge, presumably even if the offender was being supervised by a voluntary agency. This reservation was fortunately balanced by the fact that the voluntary help required by most local authorities usually includes a good deal of work of a constructional or manual nature not involving a client relationship. In general, the Working Group were convinced that the voluntary agencies could find the necessary part time community work, and where this was not always possible (and even when it was) the probation service itself should take on finding additional tasks outside the voluntary system.

Although this crucial endorsement almost guaranteed a favourable report from the Working Group it is worth recalling that there was at least one disagreement with Wootton on a matter of importance, namely, the type of order which would be required. Wootton had suggested that two types of court order could be provided for: to require community service as a condition of a probation order, or an entirely new penalty, a community service order. The Working Group came down firmly in favour of a new order, to accompany what they felt was a new form of treatment, an order incidentally which could only be issued with the offender's consent.[48] Having made this important point of principle, the Working Group considered a number of other problems, including how best to deal with breaches of community service orders, and how they might be varied if the need arose. Finally, a firm recommendation was made that the probation service should be given additional resources to match its new responsibilities and that the whole community service scheme, in line with Wootton, should be started at first on an experimental basis.[49]

The recommendations of the Wootton Report and the Working Group were accepted by the government, with certain modifications, and the Criminal Justice Act (1972) made it possible for courts to order unpaid work by offenders in the community. What the law provides in more detail is that an offender aged seventeen or over who is convicted of an offence punishable with imprisonment can, if he consents, be made subject to a Community Service Order requiring him to carry out unpaid work for a specified number of hours, not less than 40 and not more than 240. There is little doubt from the rhetoric which accompanied the passing of the Criminal Justice Act (1972) that the Community Service Order was seen as an important alternative sentence to imprisonment. The enthusiasm was tempered by caution and when community service finally got started in 1973 it was introduced, as Wootton had recommended, on an experimental basis only and was thus confined to just six areas: Durham, Inner London, Kent, Nottingham, Shropshire and South-West Lancashire. Public reaction to the experiment, and the close detail of the operation in the six areas, was monitored by the Home Office Research Unit which reported to the Home Secretary in February 1975. The Report, *Community Service Orders*, was generally favourable.[50] It pointed to a good deal of constructive press comment and came to the conclusion, after an orgy of statistics, that on balance, 'The community service experience shows that the scheme is viable; orders are being made and completed, sometimes evidently to the benefit of the offenders concerned.'[51] It was on the basis of this Report that the government extended community service to seven other areas and promised that the scheme would be further extended when other areas had made 'adequate provision for voluntary work'.

Before going on to consider RAP's several objections to Community Service Orders it is important to pause and reflect on the relatively slow progress of the idea that many more offenders might be 'treated in the community' instead of being incarcerated or closely supervised by the probation service. That the idea has been resisted so strongly is, in part, due to society's perception of the offender. For much of the present century he has been regarded as emotionally or mentally disturbed, even ill and therefore in need of a 'cure'. This has led to the professionalisation of the various treatment services, the prison service with its psychiatrists and psychologists, the probation officer trained with a psycho-analytical bias to be used in one-to-one casework situations, and so on. This professionalisation process with its esoteric and even frightening vocabulary has proved hostile to the idea that many more offenders might be 'treated in the community'. The probation service reinforced this general prejudice since it would amount to an attack on their professional status if the offender was seen to be 'cured' after a few hours work in the community under the 'wholesome influence' of volunteers.

But if the resistence of some probation officers to the organisation of community service was understandable, why was RAP critical? Surely RAP more than any other group in the penal lobby should have welcomed community service, what, then were its objections? To start with, RAP felt that not enough care was being taken to match offenders to tasks. It seemed that the probation service's major worry was always to find tasks; that, as it were, was seen as the big problem. Once it was overcome, once tasks had been found, it did not matter that much who was allocated to carry them out. Second, too few tasks did anything to develop the offender's sense of responsibility or put him into contact with other people and their problems. Third, the tasks provided were not related to the offender's community, his locality. Indeed, in this sense 'community service' was being neglected altogether. Most of these criticisms were put forward by RAP at a meeting with probation officers in London during June 1973.[52] The information on which they were based was drawn almost exclusively from the operation of community service in the Inner London area where right from the start RAP had good points of access to monitor exactly how the scheme was working out in practice. (Indeed, even before the scheme got started RAP had been in touch with the probation service and invited its members to a general meeting to discuss some of the problems which RAP felt were beginning to emerge even at the planning stage.)

RAP's tone may well have been a little too strident, but even so there is no doubt that the criticisms so far referred to contained more than an element of truth. This was later to become obvious when Inner London's experimental scheme was written up in an official document which spoke of an understaffed community service centre and offenders whose failure to carry out their Community Service Orders was 'not surprising'.[53] It is not unreasonable to emphasise that what RAP was attacking was only an experiment, a pilot scheme which would inevitably make mistakes, but mistakes which could be rectified in the future. Thus, although it might be fair to argue that the Inner London scheme was too task-orientated, lacking in a proper recognition of the offender's own preferences, this could be put right in just the same way as weaknesses in the other area experiments could be put right. RAP was far less optimistic, particularly about the way in which community service was being ordered for people who had been convicted of offences for which it was very unlikely that they would have ever been imprisoned. This had happened in Inner London and indeed, as the Home Office Research Unit was to show, in the other experimental areas as well. In this sense, the new sentence was being used to make the penal system even tougher. To suggest that Wootton had always envisaged this is hardly an argument, particularly in view of the government's apparent stress on the idea of community service as an alternative to imprisonment rather than anything else.

As if this blunt condemnation was not sufficient, RAP made two further criticisms of community service which were to effectively define it out altogether. First, there was what RAP felt to be a conflict of aims, the idea that community service could both punish and rehabilitate. For RAP this was impossible, you cannot both hurt offenders and at the same time expect to reform them. As Shaw once put it, 'if you are to punish a man retributively you must injure him. If you are to reform him, you must improve him. And men are not improved by injuries.' Second, and much more central to our main concern was RAP's claim that prisons are symbols of social control and oppression in our class-divided society and that any alternatives will serve much the same purpose:

> . . . prisons have long since lost any pretensions of leading their inmates towards a good and moral life and have stood for the past century as stark symbols of basic social control and repression. It must not be forgotten that alternative schemes produced within the present framework of society must necessarily have the same function. Community service can be looked on as that much more insidious in its approach . . . The violence and coercion of prison speaks for itself and both sides

> know where they stand. It is not so with community service – seduction has always been the liberal reformer's weapon.
>
> The values implicit in community service are bourgeois; the tasks that people are asked to undertake are tasks which will reinforce those values. In such action there is no real service to the community. To achieve this would mean revealing the inequality and injustice of society which holds the danger of further alienation for the person concerned. Yet such an attempt to view himself and his community in a realistic light must be made if an offender is to be given a radical and genuine alternative . . .
>
> To put it another way, if you work in the Home Office, then clearly it is in your interests to utilise community service to its maximum – it will be more effective than your prisons and you will attract significantly less criticism. But if you accept a radical critique of society, if you believe that it is fundamentally characterised by conflict, ridden with class divisions and dominance, then you should treat community service with much more care and subdue your liberal instincts. The 'humanity' and 'niceness' with which it is combined should not confuse the basic issues. That if we have a repressive society, it is best to have the control that is exercised out in front in the nastiness of the prison system rather than performing similar functions more effectively and wrapped up in the cotton wool of community service. Sometimes nice can be a nasty word. Beware Greeks bearing gifts. [54]

This statement, with its quasi-Marxist tone, opens up the area of fundamental disagreement between RAP and the Home Office and airs their opposing assumptions. The Home Office, broadly supporting the existing distribution of social and economic power and happy to attempt to modify criminal behaviour according to prevailing moral standards, must have realised a dialogue with RAP was unlikely to get anywhere. The Probation and Aftercare Service reached much the same conclusion, particularly after the publication of the Younger Report which RAP used to polarise opinion in an already divided service.

RAP's attitude towards the Younger Report was less pragmatic than that of the Howard League, which did not regard it as unsatisfactory but at least something to work on and improve. On the contrary, RAP came to the general conclusion that the Report amounted to little more than a 'pernicious reorganisation' of existing punishments masquerading under the banner of liberal reform. [55] The Custody and Control Order (CCO) was particularly objectionable. It meant that the prisoner would be subject to a form of indeterminate sentence; when he was to be released into the community to serve the remainder of his sentence on licence would be decided by a local advisory committee. RAP regarded the indeterminate sentence as an infringement of the young offender's civil liberties. But more than that, it was probable that the local advisory committees would be dominated by 'establishment interests' reacting like the Parole Board, that is, with massive caution. Crucially, these objections were added to by a condemnation of the powers which Younger recommended were necessary to supervise the young offender on licence. What the Report argued was that the Secretary of State should be empowered to 'provide a wide range of requirements' referring to such things as place of residence, nature of work, avoidance of certain places of resort and so on. It seems that the objective was 'total supervision', an objective which was far from the probation officer's traditional role which was to 'advise, assist and befriend'. With the range of powers recommended by Younger no one would be advising, assisting or befriending anyone, control was the new idea and a very rigid form of control at that. RAP extended a similar criticism to the non-custodial Supervision and Control Order which also envisaged 'strict control'. In one way the Supervision and Control Orders were even more unacceptable than CCOs in that they contained the by now notorious provision enabling probation officers to apply to a local magistrate for the temporary detention of their clients for a period of up to 72 hours. The fact that this was to be used not only if the Supervision and Control Order had been breached, but also in situations where the probation officer simply thought that it might be breached, convinced RAP that the 72 hour detention order was so outrageous that it would never be implemented. On the question of custodial establishments RAP felt that Younger had simply engaged in an exercise in semantics. The recommendation that young persons prisons, borstals and detention centres should be merged into something called a 'neighbourhood' establishment would change nothing; it was just the emperor appearing in new clothes.

The Younger Report's recommendation for Custody and Control Orders was leaked to the press shortly before the National Association of Probation Officers' (NAPO) annual conference at Weymouth early in May 1974. The result was a major conference row, and it is of interest that the details of the row were reported in RAP's June Newsletter by Neil Patrick, a member of RAP's West Yorkshire branch. West Yorkshire RAP was centred in Bradford and had been formed early in 1974. As probation officers, its organising nucleus claimed easy access to NAPO forums and in particular NMAG, the NAPO Members Action Group which had been started in 1972 by probation officers who felt frustrated by the alleged 'inactivity and incompetence' of the traditional NAPO.[56] Neil Patrick supported NMAG and had published at least one article on RAP in its 'pirate' magazine, *PROBE.*[57] (This was entirely appropriate since among NMAG's statement of aims is a firm commitment to abolish imprisonment of offenders other than those who present a grave risk to society.) What Patrick had to say about the Weymouth conference is relevant on two counts. In the first place, he pointed out that although it was a RAP member who had proposed a radical resolution calling on NAPO to withhold social enquiry reports until guilt had been proved, this in itself was not enough. It was a mere symbol of the sort of links which RAP must quickly establish with the probation service, especially its younger members who were active in NMAG. Second, he claimed that many reservations were expressed about Younger's recommendation for Custody and Control Orders. Further, although a resolution stating that NAPO would be unwilling to operate such orders unless they were supported at a general meeting of the association was lost by a mere three votes, 'simply due to the content of the resolution', the meeting 'overwhelmingly condemned these new measures'.[58] This claim was contested by NAPO's hierarchy. A letter to RAP from the chairman of the Association's Parliamentary and Public Relations Committee argued that probation officers had varied in their responses to Younger, from total rejection to total acceptance. To claim as Patrick had done that the conference had 'overwhelmingly condemned' the Report was simply untrue, indeed no resolution to that effect had ever been debated, the resolution in question, the one that was lost, had only called upon the association 'not to accept any changes' as a result of the Report unless they are supported by a majority vote at a general meeting. This rejoinder was firm, but not without some gesture towards conciliation. [59] The same can hardly be said of Mr Kenneth Howe's response. As NPAO's chairman he did little to hide his contempt for what Patrick had written.[60]

In a spirited reply to his critics (published by RAP) Patrick was unrepentent.[61] The details of his defence are unimportant. What is significant though, is that soon after the Weymouth affair RAP was publicly informed that its active involvement with NAPO had very definite limits. During 1974 and the early part of 1975 it appears that NAPO's Social Policy Committee devoted several meetings to an appraisal of the Association's relationship with other groups in the penal lobby. The conclusion it reached was that it would be unwise for the Association to become too closely involved with groups like RAP or PROP. Two reasons were given in support of this conclusion. First, NAPO had statutory obligations and this set it apart from groups like RAP and PROP, both in terms of structure as well as procedure. Second, NAPO had to be selective in its cooperation with other groups, and if it wanted to pursue its dialogue with the Prison Officers Association it could not be seen in an alliance with RAP and PROP at the same time; the POA would find this intolerable.[62] Although these reasons are faithful to NAPO's establishment bias they are hardly explicit about why RAP was really defined out, that is, how NAPO's hierarchy regarded RAP's stand on Younger as not only one guaranteed to divide the Association, but also one which was calculated to widen what was an already identifiable gap between those younger officers who regarded themselves as agents of social change and those older officers who saw themselves as agents of social control. That this gap existed at all was partly as a consequence of the shift towards a sociological rather than a psychological approach to casework. This led to a much more critical look at society itself. The question was asked: why should the probation officer spend time psycho-analysing or self-determining his deprived client, acting like a first aid worker treating symptoms while the disease itself, an unequal society which discriminates against the weak and the poor, is allowed to go unchecked when surely what the probation officer really needs is a political commitment to bring about radical social change? It was just this sort of political dimension which divided many young probation officers from NAPO's hierarchy, and it was a division which RAP's activities were bound to reinforce.

It would be wrong to think that this is all that has divided NAPO in the seventies. There were other serious problems such as the erosion of the traditional independence of the front-line probation officer. With the rapid expansion of the service there has grown up a management structure which means that many important decisions are now ultimately the responsibility of senior officers with no direct knowledge of the clients concerned. It is easy to understand that this is resented and it was an important contributing factor in the revolt over Younger since the Report made it clear that the new Orders it recommended were to be effectively controlled by senior staff, albeit in consultation with front-line officers. It seemed to a NMAG member that a corollary of growing control over clients was an increase in the control over front-line probation officers.[63] Coupled with this very real anxiety and the development of an increasingly well-defined hierarchy there was, and to some extent there still is, a feeling that NAPO has failed to look after its members' economic interests, that it is somehow an old fashioned 'professional association' quite unsuited to the tough environment of collective bargaining. Young probation officers are especially critical of NAPO in this context and there have been several calls for a new orientation, including proposals for an amalgamation with NALGO.

It would be wrong, then, to see the struggle within NAPO as being entirely about 'change' versus 'control'. On the other hand, the political implications of that particular aspect of the struggle were by no means lost on NAPO's official leadership. After all, it was the Association's chairman who expressed the anxiety that, 'In plain terms, radical social change can appear indistinguishable from subversion.'[64] To the extent that RAP was plainly subversive, its involvement in NAPO had to be curtailed.

If RAP was in trouble with the probation service in 1974 and 1975 it was on no better terms with its sponsor, Christian Action. The relationship between RAP and Christian Action has never been an easy one. There have been financial strains and it is difficult to believe therefore that its support can go on for ever; eventually RAP will be asked to leave and find a home and cash elsewhere.

Christian Action would also like to get rid of RAP for political reasons. In the first place, and most obviously perhaps, RAP is far too radical for Christian Action's governing Council. True, Canon Collins started Christian Action as a fellowship, to achieve radical social and economic change, but it is hard to think that its Council, composed as it is of busy public worthies and nominees from the established churches, is really in the same radical league as RAP. Second, Christian Action has always been worried that RAP would threaten its legal status as a registered charity. In theory at least, registered charities are not allowed to engage in political activity, to campaign for example to change the law. That this is an apparent absurdity is illustrated by the knowledge that the Howard League for Penal Reform is a registered charity. As Benedict Nightingale has remarked, the very name would now appal the Charity Commissioners.[65] However, the fact that some groups who do engage in political activities have been successfully registered as charities does not alter the fact that plenty of other groups, Amnesty, NCCL, for example, have not been, and this is a constant threat to Christian Action since the financial benefits of being a registered charity are considerable. In this situation it is no wonder that those charities who 'flirt' with political activity are cautious. It is equally understandable, that they should demand reform of the charity law which is surely political in itself in that it acts as a defence of the *status quo*. There is plenty of public support for reform and the Charity Law Reform Committee has gone so far as to suggest an entirely new type of organisation, the Non-Profit Distributing Organisation (NPDO).[66] The idea is simple: NPDOs would be entitled to all the advantages of charities, but with no restrictions placed on political activities. The only control over their operations would take the form of strict regulations to ensure that none of the assets and untaxed income are spirited away into private hands.

To suggest a reform is one thing, to get it through is quite another, and it seems likely that Christian Action will have to live with the charity law as it stands for some time to come. It has coped successfully so far, but RAP in particular has given it some very anxious moments. Shortly after RAP became a full time project, for example, it was given a complete issue of the *Christian Action Journal* to make out its case for alternatives to prison. This duly appeared in the summer of 1972. In the main it seems to have been well received, with the exception of an intellectually imaginative article on 'Political RAP'.[67] Presented as twelve points the argument in this unsigned article stressed that capitalism was a problem culture, that criminal law was defined in the interests of the rich and against the poor and quoted Marx to the effect that individuals should not be punished for their crimes, rather, we should destroy those conditions which lead to crime. In the next issue of the *Christian Action Journal* RAP had to publish a disclaimer, arguing that the unsigned article did not represent its official policy, and any confusion was regretted.[68] As Christian Action was neurotic about its charitable status, and because RAP still had to sidestep the Inland Revenue's watching brief, this disclaimer was a sensible tactic.

In what can be best described as an on-going anxiety over Christian Action's charitable status RAP has injected a note of scepticism. The idea is that the Charity Commissioners are used as the bogeymen which the Council wheel out when RAP takes up a truly radical stance. In other words, Christian Action does not really approve of RAP's radical politics (or its tactics) and the charity law has been used as a devious means of exercising control. What truth there is in this interpretation is a matter for argument but it is certain that RAP, for whatever reason, has been taken to task by Christian Action over what is permissible under the charity law, and to this extent at least the law has placed limits on its political activities.

There were no such problems when RAP busied itself with organising specific alternative projects to imprisonment. Indeed, to the extent that RAP could actually be seen to be 'doing good' in the community Christian Action welcomed its involvement, however aggressive. In the early days though, RAP's progress on this front was cautious and directed mainly at expanding an existing alternative project which, by January 1972, was already well underway in Fulham.[69], started by a former prison visitor, Jean Davies, this project involved employing ex-prisoners to make jewellery. RAP's initiative was simply to expand the whole enterprise and the available evidence suggests that RAP was firmly committed to this expansion.

Given such a firm commitment it was disappointing that in the final analysis RAP's initiative came to very little. For one reason or another it was left for Jean Davies to go her own way and RAP pioneered its own alternative project at Excell House, a modest property which was acquired through Christian Action from Lambeth Council. After a lot of repair and decorating work, funded mainly by Christian Action, Excell House finally got underway as an experimental type hostel where it was hoped that the ex-offender/recidivist and others could learn to live together as a self-regulating community. RAP was particularly anxious that there should be no well-defined sense of hierarchy at Excell, no warder writing his own rigid rules for others to follow. Instead, the 'you are the authority' model was to be followed with group meetings where decisions would be made along the lines of a 'democratic family'. The whole project was based on the 'principle of helping people who can respond to a non-authoritarian regime and also given the opportunity can be of constructive use to the community within the home and possibly find a more self-fulfilling role for themselves in the community outside.' [70] Given a participating community at Excell, and one which worked outwards by starting local community projects, the ex-offender/recidivist would come to realise a more constructive potential, and one in which prison had no place.

The idea behind Excell House was an idealistic one which was also very difficult to achieve in practice. At one point the community folded up altogether and RAP had to give much more detailed consideration to exactly what sort of regime was required. Whether or not the new regime was in any way more successful is difficult to say, but it is certain that after a short spell with another Christian Action project Excell House was finally closed down in the summer of 1976. Fortunately RAP was committed to exploring other alternatives, and in the provisions of the Criminal Justice Act (1972) it found just what it wanted, or so it seemed, the deferred sentence.

In fact, people on deferred sentences, i.e. those at risk, had originally been thought suitable for Excell House, but it was not until the Newham Alternatives Project got underway in the summer of 1974 that RAP really became involved in operating the deferred sentence as a specific enterprise. What the Criminal Justice Act (1972) provided for was that a Crown Court or a Magistrates Court could defer passing sentence on an offender to take into account some expected change in his circumstances which might reasonably set him on the right road. For example, a convicted offender might plead that he has the offer of a new job lined up and that this will make all the difference to his prospects. In circumstances such as this, if the offender consents, the Judge or Magistrate can defer passing sentence for a period of up to six months. At the end of the specified period the offender returns to court where he is sentenced, bearing in mind how he has behaved in the meantime. At no point can the deferment be curtailed unless the offender commits another offence. Strictly speaking, no formal conditions are specified but as already indicated the court must have reason to believe that the offender's circumstances are likely to change for the better. In very simple terms, the Newham Alternatives Project hoped to be a significant factor in those changed circumstances, a centre offering support and advice which would help offenders 'get themselves together' and pull out of the downward spiral to prison.

RAP's choice of Newham was to some extent forced. Originally the project had been planned for Islington, a borough with lots of community schemes which RAP hoped its referrals might get involved in. This location was unacceptable to the Home Office since Community Service Orders had just been introduced into Inner London and RAP's presence in Islington would simply complicate things.[71] Another and more obvious objection was raised when RAP thought of starting its project in Waltham Forest. The local probation service was organising its own alternatives scheme which would make use of the deferred sentence, so RAP's project was therefore unnecessary. After more enquiries the choice seems to have narrowed between Redbridge and Newham and, finally, RAP settled for Newham. There is no doubt that RAP took on a tough borough, with bad housing, high unemployment rate and, crucially for RAP, in 1970 a serious crime rate 5 per cent higher than the average for England and Wales. If RAP wanted to put its alternative project to a stiff test then Newham was clearly the place to be. But if the location had been decided what about official permission, and in particular, the attitude of the Home Office? Negotiations with the Home Office took a long time. Initially the civil servants concerned were unhelpful, promising to write but then not doing so. This was a constant anxiety for RAP since by the summer of 1973 the Cadbury Trust was showing a keen interest in funding the project but it wanted Home Office support and a directive from the Lord Chancellor's Office asking the courts to cooperate. RAP kept pushing, stressing the limitations involved in other alternatives to prison; the class barriers associated with probation, the apparent inability of Community Service Orders to provide anything other than manual labour, and so on. The Newham Alternatives Project was argued on what appeared to be its strengths, its commitment to involve working class people as helpers, its intention to cater for the individual offender, to 'fix up an alternative tailor-made for his or her particular needs.'[72] RAP's persistence eventually paid off, the Home Office dropped its objections and with assistance from the local council which provided a short-life property in Forest Gate the Newham Alternatives Project was ready to start, with the apparent cooperation of both the courts and the local probation service.

The way NAP acquired referrals was simple. If a probation officer felt that a defendant was likely to be sent to prison, borstal or detention centre he could consider recommending him to NAP. If he felt, having due regard to the defendant's record, that this would be a good idea he could suggest to the court that a deferred sentence (in association with NAP) would be the most appropriate 'disposal'. Before this stage was reached NAP, through the probation officer, would have already spoken to the defendant, explaining exactly what NAP was about and pointing out that there was no compulsion to accept a referral, he could simply 'try for NAP' if he felt it would be to his benefit. NAP visited the defendant in his own home or, if necessary, in custody, accompanied by a Newham probation officer or a prison welfare officer. The requirement of an 'accompanying officer' was firmly laid down by the Home Office. When the deferment period was coming to an end NAP wrote its report for the court together with the participant, and then discussed it with the probation officer who had originally made the referral. In most cases NAP asked the court to give a conditional discharge.[73]

To summarise exactly what NAP did for its referrals is not easy. A literacy project was started, a women's group met at the Mayflower Settlement in the south of the borough and there was a fairly successful therapy group on Tuesdays. The level of commitment to these activities varied and their significance should not be overestimated since what NAP seems to have become was not so much a centre providing 'specific things to do' but rather just a friendly place in the locality where referrals could go for support and advice as and when they needed it.[74] This is not to suggest that NAP's referrals were entirely free to come and go as they pleased, though it must be said that only a few of them were really pressed to attend on a regular basis if they seemed to be coping on their own.

It may have been this easy going approach which upset the

probation service. Some probation officers did not use NAP at all while many others were far from friendly. There were other contributory factors though, not least being the conviction among some officers that penal institutions were not as bad as RAP made them out to be and that offenders would be better off inside than being looked after by a bunch of amateurs. The fact that the amateurs were mainly women was seen as a further limitation and probation officers were unwilling to refer potentially dangerous offenders.[75] This was perhaps understandable, but not quite so acceptable was the probation service's apparent reluctance, in the early days at least, to refer offenders who were likely to be imprisoned; all they had in mind were offenders who were heading for a fine or probation. NAP had to fight very hard on this crucial point, it was an alternative to prison and not a substitute for a fine or probation. It seems that when faced with a court which was anticipating a prison sentence probation officers were unwilling to threaten their credibility by recommending what appeared to the bench as a 'soft option'. The tensions between NAP and the probation service made cooperation difficult, and it is clear that NAP sought to step outside of its dependent relationship with the service by asking lawyers to refer cases, and sometimes NAP workers went so far as to sit in on local courts to pick up new cases that way.[76] The need for these tactics aside, though, it is worth making the point that some probation officers, particularly younger ones, supported NAP and worked very hard to make it a success.

The attitude of local magistrates was predictable. In theory NAP was welcome. Indeed, when the project started the Chief Clerk to Newham's magistrates went so far as to give it his public support.[77] Unfortunately the Chief Clerk's enthusiasm was not shared by the local bench. NAP made several attempts to engage Newham magistrates in a dialogue about the penal system but its approaches were largely ignored. For example, at a teach-in on alternatives at a local mission only five out of Newham's seventy-six magistrates even bothered to attend. Letters to two 'hard line' magistrates were ignored, presumably they had no interest in a meeting with NAP and their refusal to even reply was perhaps intended to make this clear. [78] The Crown Court judges were apparently more open to argument and after a meeting with NAP the three permanent judges at the Snaresbrook Crown Court agreed to consider deferring a sentence if it was recommended by the probation officer concerned. The difficulty here was the Crown Court circuit system which meant that all too frequently NAP workers found themselves up against a judge who knew nothing about their project. In situations like this they had very little pull, to give a sketchy outline about how NAP might help the offender was rarely convincing.

In spite of all these difficulties NAP can claim to have been a success. This at least is what the statistics indicate. Between August 1974 and July 1976 the total number of offenders who got a deferred sentence to NAP was forty. Of these eighteen received a conditional discharge at the end of their deferment, six a fine, three probation, three a suspended sentence, one a Community Service Order and four were committed to prison or borstal. The outcome of the remaining five cases had still to be decided when NAP reported. True, this is not the whole story and there were quite clearly failures. For example, in eighteen cases involving NAP no deferred sentence was given and the offenders were sent to prison, borstal or detention.[79] On balance though NAP would claim to have done a good job, kept a significant number of offenders out of prison and saved the Prison Department hard cash. It was this cash aspect of the project, the fact that alternatives were far cheaper than prison, that *The Guardian* chose to highlight in a sympathetic article on NAP in December 1975, 'Spending freeze boosts alternatives to prison'.[80]

If NAP meant some relief for the Prison Department and satisfied Christian Action by showing RAP's willingness to do something practical, it was also a project which led to internal disagreements since it seemed to rest on premises which at other times RAP would want to reject. The disagreements were important and they will shortly be considered in some detail. In the meantime, and by way of contrast, RAP's policy on children in trouble is worth considering since that, at least, was unequivocal.

The problems of children in trouble were occupying most groups in the penal lobby by the mid 1970s. The reason for this in one sense is simple enough: overcrowded juvenile institutions. But had not the 1969 Children and Young Persons Act floated the idea of intermediate treatment to help the social worker in his new supervisory role and as a way of keeping children out of custodial institutions? This was indeed the case, but very little was done along these lines and it was even argued as late as 1975 that the idea of community based intermediate treatment was still vague, a conceptual vacuum which local authorities seemed unwilling to fill. Given such a negative response it was perhaps not surprising that custodial institutions for the young were at bursting point. This pressure had certain sensational repercussions, for example, really disruptive children can be detained in 'secure units' which are funded by both the government and local authorities. It became increasingly obvious during the 1970s that the demand for places in 'secure units' was outstripping the supply and as a consequence a number of really disruptive children had to be detained in prison. This fact, the knowledge that a fourteen year old girl might spend time in Holloway, caught the headlines. The clamour for more secure units grew in intensity; children in Holloway or any prison was intolerable, however disruptive they might be. There is no doubt that the public row over 'secure units' did much to turn the spotlight on children in trouble, but in some ways it turned the focus away from alternatives to custody, which was surely the central issue and not, however grim, the plight of a minority. As David Thorpe put it:

> Intermediate treatment, in its less intense forms, is a good preventive measure and in its highly intensive form constitutes an alternative to residential care. To focus on the need for secure accommodation for the very small minority of persistent juvenile offenders is to court disaster for the majority of medium-range delinquents who at present seem to risk unnecessary and eventually very damaging institutionalisation. [81]

Thorpe's contribution was one of many in the on-going debate sparked off by what was considered to be the failure of the 1969 Children and Young Persons Act or, more correctly, the failure of the authorities to implement its provisions to the full. To some extent RAP joined in this debate at very practical levels, pointing out that the Act had never really been given a chance and in its written evidence to the Social Services Subcommittee of the Expenditure Committee of the House of Commons it referred to 'lack of resources' and inadequate rewards for those who 'undertake the exacting work of intervening in crisis situations.' [82] However, RAP's interest in the operation of the 1969 Act had very definite limits. For example, there is no evidence that it investigated how social workers were developing their supervisory functions under the Act, or that it considered how this, in conjunction with the failure to develop intermediate treatment, might have contributed to an increase in the number of children in custody. Such questions were not central to RAP, for it was more concerned with an attempt to see the problems of children and the law in their wider political context. It was this context that RAP had explored in its pamphlet, *Children Out of Trouble.* [83]

Children Out of Trouble had a very simple message. We live in a class divided society. The gap between the rich and the poor is as great now as it was at certain times in the nineteenth century, a situation which is apparently acceptable in our present day democracy because of the hegemonic domination of the ruling class:

> Our social class structure is extremely resistant to change. We have the paradox of a parliamentary democracy with fairly strong roots in teh consciousness of all classes which lessens the danger of authoritarian political control, but where class domination is so habitual that only a few people are fully conscious of it. The people with power and influence have all from the first been highly privileged, with freedom to move, think, study and have realisable ambitions . . . The chasm between rich and poor, privileged and deprived in terms of the chance to make a choice, to exercise a talent, is as great now as in Disraeli's time, and the basis of this difference is now, as it was then, economic.[84]

The connection between this and children in trouble is clear: such children are the victims of our unequal society and their alleged 'crimes' little more than a response to their politically induced deprivation. To concentrate on the 'nuts and bolts' of the 1969 Children and Young Persons Act is to obscure the root cause of juvenile delinquency and the huge structural changes which are needed to attack a growing social problem. True, there is no simple relationship between poverty and crime and so structural change when it comes 'would not abolish crime – a totally different social order alone can do that – but it would alleviate some of the worst economic deprivation, and might therefore lessen crime to some extent'.[85] The implications of this analysis hardly need spelling out and whereas the Home Office was prepared to listen to a 'nuts and bolts' critique of its legislation for children in trouble it showed no interest in a critique which challenged its fundamental assumptions and posited a radical alternative. A review of *Children Out of Trouble* in *New Society* made much the same point:

> It seems a pity . . . that the RAP document puts forward not a single constructive idea for improving the legal framework within which delinquency is managed. The ultimate answer may lie in social revolution or 'destroying the apparatus of the judicial process' as they advocate. But for the present they are unlikely to find many takers for that view, and certainly not in the circles that create policy.[86]

Never it seems has *New Society* been more right! RAP's political message simply fell on stony ground, buried presumably beneath a landslide of 'constructive' ideas. But if the Home Office could cheerfully sidestep RAP on children in trouble it could not so easily ignore what it had to say on control units.

The introduction of control units was more or less a direct response to the prison riots of 1972. Speaking at the Annual Conference of the Prison Officers Association in May 1973 the Association's chairman argued that in the major prison 'incidents' since 1968 'the same nucleus of prisoners kept cropping up with monotonous regularity'. [87] These 'aggressive psychopaths' were seen by the chairman as troublemakers; they contaminated other long term prisoners and provoked disturbances and riots. Only by removing this nucleus of troublemakers to a separate and highly secure prison could the trend towards disruption be stopped. This suggestion was considered by the then Home Secretary, Mr Robert Carr, but turned down for the following reasons. First, given that most of the prisoners would be, almost be definition, violent and manipulative, the risk of disruption would be high, too high in fact for the authorities to contemplate without having tried out other solutions first. Second, putting all the troublemakers together would create a human timebomb and to expect prison officers to wait for its almost certain explosion was asking too much. Third, it would be difficult to avoid the impression that a special prison would be seen as the end of the road, a sort of repressive dustbin. The prisoners would be thought of as being beyond reform and consequently the prison staff would become guards pure and simple, their only function being to keep the lid firmly on the dustbin. There could be no job satisfaction for prison officers in a set-up like this, so where, asked the Home Secretary, would the staff come from? [88]

But if the Home Secretary was unsympathetic to the idea of a special prison for the so-called troublemakers he was at pains to emphasise agreement with the Prison Officers Association that a disruptive nucleus could be identified and that steps should be taken to control it without delay. To this end he made a number of specific proposals which included the introduction of a number of 'secure cells' in local prisons and the extension of segregation units to all dispersal prisons holding high risk prisoners. These units had been recommended in the Radzinowicz Report and were designed to provide a 'sharp inducement to wrongdoers to mend their ways'. [89] The basic regime was harsh and normal prison privileges were withdrawn. Four of the existing dispersal prisons already had segregation units. The Home Secretary proposed a fifth at Wakefield, eventually completing the series at Gartree. As if these additions to[the repressive apparatus were not enough, Robert Carr went on to announce the setting up of two control units, each capable of holding between thirty and forty men at any given time. The function of these units was explicitly to accommodate, as necessary, this small group of intractable troublemakers. There was, presumably, to be a progression, that is, control units would be more repressive than segregation units. But how, in more precise terms, would the regimes differ? If segregation units were tough, in what ways would control units be tougher? These questions remained unanswered. All the Home Secretary would say in public was that as prisoners might sometimes stay in control units for long periods their allocation to the units and their release would be centrally controlled. As for the details of the regime, they were still being worked out.

Clearly, the Home Office, as it later claimed, made no secret of its intention to build control units, a Parliamentary reply from the Home Secretary on 11 May 1973 substantiates this point[90] , and it did not refuse to disclose where the units were to be located for these details were announced in Parliament on 28 January 1974.[91] Finally, the grand opening date was formally declared by the new Home Secretary Roy Jenkins on 24 July 1974.[92] As proper and straightforward as all this may seem, what the Home Office did not make public, and which was crucial, was the precise nature of the control unit regime. This only began to leak out as the result of a report by the *Sunday Times'* Insight teams on one of the control unit's first victims, Michael Williams.[93] It was this disclosure that forced the Home Office to show its hand, to reveal in public the precise nature of the control units regime.

According to a document received by RAP the regime is divided into two phases, each normally lasting for an expected minimum period of ninety days. During the first phase the emphasis is on separation from other prisoners. Any work done, any educational or leisure activities are carried on in the prisoner's cell. He is isolated there for twenty-three hours a day. During the one remaining hour he can exercise and 'share worship' with other prisoners. This association apart, the prisoner is on his own. Even his contact with the prison staff is deliberately restricted. This is to avoid confrontation, or to make the prisoner's existence more intolerable, the emphasis is optional. If the prisoner misbehaves, say argues with a prison officer, shouts or breaks things, he reverts to day one, no matter how long he has already served. The second phase allows for a 'measure' of activity with other prisoners in the control unit. To some extent, then, the prisoner is allowed to work and relax in the company of others. The purpose of this relaxation is purely functional from the prison authorities' point of view in that it enables them to test whether the prisoner has learned to cooperate and mix with other prisoners without 'causing trouble'.

The Home Office made no pretence that the control units regime was anything other than punitive, any 'treatment effects' were regarded as a bonus. There was clearly no such bonus for Michael Williams and the public clamour against his punishment quickly turned into a campaign to abolish control units altogether. RAP played a significant part in this campaign, its first major contribution coming in November when it organised a public meeting on control units at the London School of Economics and Political Science for delegates to the Labour Party Conference.[94]

This meeting was only one of many public protests against the control units. Indeed, even before it had been held the Home Secretary had already been forced to modify the regime in two important ways. First, he proposed to introduce an independent element into the allocation procedure. Any request to transfer a prisoner to a control unit would be referred to the board of visitors of the holding prison, and transfers would be allowed against its view only with the Home Secretary's permission. Second, there were to be changes in the type of misbehaviour taken into consideration when referring a prisoner back to day one of the regime, and the reference back was no longer to be automatic. These modifications were regarded as diversionary and RAP demanded total abolition, organising a demonstration outside Wormwood Scrubs on 14 December 1974 to reinforce this demand. This was reasonably well reported in the press, but RAP was far from pleased with the support it had received from certain organisations in the Control Units Action Group, though this disappointment perhaps showed a little naivete. CUAG had been formed in October 1974. Its membership, apart from RAP, was NCCL, NACRO, the Howard League, PROP, Prisoners' Families and Friends Association, MIND, Up Against the Law and the Prisoners' Wives Union. Right from the start these very different organisations found it almost impossible to cooperate. When CUAG's original policy statement, for example, which included the demand to return Michael Williams to the normal prison routine and an end to any further allocations to the Wakefield control unit, was issued to the press, the Howard League made some comments to *The Guardian* in which, RAP felt, the statement was distorted.[95] RAP was furious and what had been an uneasy alliance finally crumbled when the Howard League was asked to leave CUAG early in 1975.[96] From then on CUAG was effectively dead, and the more moderate groups like NACRO and NCCL broke away and campaigned on their own.

It would be wrong, though, to think that the Howard League's ill-advised comments to the press caused CUAG's failure. There was much more to the argument than just that, and not least was RAP's suspicion that the Howard League was soft-pedalling on the question of control units, unable or even unwilling to take a firm stand against the Prison Department and the Home Office. Why the League's Director Martin Wright chose to run the risk of alienating CUAG by seeming to blur the issue is clear. In the first place, he genuinely believed that a public slanging match would only stiffen official resolve; the Prison Department would only respond favourably to restrained and sympathetic protest. Second, the Howard League's close relationship with the bureaucracy was again at stake, and the League was not prepared to risk this relationship by attending public demonstrations or by supporting protest meetings which conducted the campaign against control units in the wider political context of a capitalist system which 'inherently promotes the interests of the property owning class' and 'deliberately creates a deprived minority'. [97] This was not the Howard League's context by far and CUAG's failure was to this extent inevitable.

The ill-feeling generated by CUAG's internal wrangling was quickly forgotten in October 1975 when the Home Secretary announced that the use of control units was to be discontinued, or at least that was what most groups in the penal lobby thought he had announced. [98] In a written reply Mr Jenkins reminded the House that control units had been set up by his predecessor to cope with troublesome prisoners who made life unbearable for both staff and other prisoners. He made no attempt to criticise this decision, nor indeed did he believe that there was anything in the allegations that control units were brutal and cruel in that they involved sensory deprivation. He pointed out that since the Wakefield unit had been opened only six prisoners had been allocated to it. No doubt this was a tribute to the prison staff's professionalism but, in terms of staff and other resources, six referrals did not justify the unit's existence and the Home Secretary therefore directed that no further prisoners should be admitted to it, except those who themselves request removal from association under the provisions of rule 43. This seemed to be an official climbdown. Little attention was paid to the last paragraph of the Home Secretary's reply which said that the option to use 'the accommodation' would be retained 'for those who have to be segregated from the ordinary prison population under the same rule 43, but in the interests of good order and discipline.' This apparent 'double-talk' was largely ignored. As *The Guardian* was later to comment, 'Although Mr Jenkins suggested in Parliament that it was possible the units could be reopened should the disciplinary need arise, his statement was widely interpreted as a retreat from an unfortunate experiment by the Home Office.'[99] To put the same thing another way, faced with an angry Prison Officers Association the Home Secretary's ambiguity, his apparent concession to retain the control units 'just in case' was a tactical necessity, but that was all. RAP was far less charitable. The Home Secretary had apparently given similar assurances in February 1975, assurances which were soon broken, what reason was there to expect that he would act any differently now? In any case, in retaining control units for segregation under rule 43, what were the Home Secretary's intentions? Was segregation to become tougher – 'control under another name' became the slogan – or was his use of the term accommodation very specific, with the intention to keep the buildings and ditch the regime? There were too many unanswered questions, and this was a feature of the control units campaign. Finding out exactly what was happening inside the Wakefield unit or entering into the dialogue between civil servants and politicians, initiatives like these were almost impossible for RAP. For example, the BBC's Man Alive team did a programme on control units in May 1976. This included filmed contributions from ex-prisoners like John Masterson, the first inmate to be released having spent time in a control unit. The remainder of the programme was apparently taken up by a discussion between the former Home Secretary Robert Carr and various members of the Prison Department. RAP tried to get somebody outside of the 'prison service and its apologists' to participate in the programme but this was refused.[100] The Prison Department was presumably feeling hard done by over the question of control units and it is extremely doubtful if it would have agreed to participate in a programme which included a radical group like RAP. Other groups were treated more sympathetically by the Prison Department. The Howard League, for example, was allowed to inspect the control unit and its Director and Chairman later met the Home Secretary to express their concern.[101]

The extent to which these various pressures shifted government policy is genuinely difficult to say since what actually happens inside our prisons is surrounded by secrecy, a secrecy which is well served by the ambiguity of official statements. To say that the control unit regime is now defunct would be far too bold; more stringent segregation under rule 43 might indeed amount to little more than 'control under another name', who is to say otherwise? But even more important, the control unit experiment reveals yet again that the prison system is not only arbitrary and protected from democratic scrutiny, it is also becoming increasingly geared to modifying human behaviour in totally unacceptable ways. For the penal lobby the anxious question remains, what next?[102]

Notes on strategy

RAP was out to abolish prisons. Thus, reforms which simply improved prison conditions might be thought of as laudable and even humanitarian, but they were not RAP's concern. For RAP the stress was on abolition. Almost from the start, this was RAP's uncompromising position and it caused great anxiety among certain reform groups, most notably the Howard League whose Director wrote to RAP asking:

> Even if you think that you can get prisons abolished within ten years, which is unlikely, ought you not to try to make things more endurable to those who remain inside during those years? Or should penal reformers have left things exactly as they were?
>
> Because there have been improvements in prison conditions over the last 100 years: the abolition of the crank and the treadmill, the silence rule, the prison haircut, and many other atrocities. God knows there is a long way to go; but are you really saying that one should not try to reform these things? [103]

This challenge did not shift RAP from its position. Reforms, however laudable and humanitarian, were none of its business. If groups like the Howard League wanted to press on with reforms all well and good, RAP would not be tempted, its focus would remain firmly on abolition. Much the same response was evident when PROP was formed in 1972. PROP was welcome because it asserted 'the rights of prisoners to humane conditions'[104], but any reforms it might win have little to do with the struggle for abolition.

This response to groups like the Howard League and PROP over the question of reforms can be regarded as fairly neutral but it was not the only possible response. Equally plausible, and it seems implicit in much of RAP's critique of the Howard League, was the suggestion that reforms simply reinforce the system, the idea that by improving conditions prisons are made more acceptable, they are legitimised in the public mind. To the extent that RAP's critique of the League implied this the relationship between the two groups was anything but neutral, it was openly bitter. PROP's reformist strategy was seen to hold much the same dangers. RAP was not as hostile to PROP as it was to the Howard League for a number of obvious reasons, nonetheless, and as we have already shown, RAP placed very definite limits on its cooperation with the prisoners' movement.

Although RAP was right to be cautious about reform its analysis was far too crude, it failed to distinguish, in Mathiesen's terms, between positive and negative reforms[105], i.e. reforms which would support the prison system and reforms which would undermine it, eventually leading to its abolition. This distinction, then, allows for a link, a continuum between reform and abolition. An example of a positive reform would be the call for more prison psychiatrists and psychologists. This would reinforce the prison system's apparatus of social control and still further confirm its legitimacy as a treatment system. The public would continue to think of the criminal as being diseased or ill and in need of treatment. A negative reform would be to demand the abolition of mail censorship as a means of developing links between the expelled and the world outside, in this way the repression and futility of the prison system could be exposed for all to see. The prison authorities could no longer hide behind the barrier of secrecy.

RAP's failure to make the distinction between positive and negative reforms, its inability or apparent unwillingness to realise that not all reforms support the prison system limited its activities to a very narrow base. For example, in the past the Howard League has called for both more psychiatrists/psychologists and the lifting of mail censorship. There is no reason why RAP should not have campaigned with the League on the latter while at the same time opposing the former. Similar tactical cooperation was surely possible with other groups, PROP in particular. Reforms need not be the conservative force that RAP had always assumed. RAP's problem was that it began life so anxious to avoid becoming a pale shadow of the Howard League that it eschewed reform altogether. True, such an extreme tactic was short lived and there is evidence that by 1975 RAP was openly supporting a range of negative reforms which would have made the prison system more open. However, the worrying aspect of this strategic turnabout is that it lacked any reasoned justification. It is almost as if the call to lift mail censorship, for example, was stumbled upon by accident, a casual reform which is seen in no way as different from all other reforms. Without a firm grasp of the distinctions that need to be made RAP's foray into reform could be more perilous than its previous isolation.[106] As Mathiesen points out, the embrace of positive reform is always there, such reforms are always on offer from the prison authorities.[107] To take them up would be a fateful decision, and RAP must be more keenly aware about what is at stake. It would be comforting to think that this apparent lack of awareness or clarity was simply tactical, that RAP did not want to be identified by the prison authorities as an abolition group working to undermine the system from within, supporting only those negative reforms which would bring this about. This would be a plausible tactic, but it is not one that RAP has consciously adopted.

It might be thought that RAP's appreciation of the distinction between positive and negative reforms saved it from a radical paralysis. RAP started out to abolish prisons, knowing that the process would be a long one. It did not believe that the prison system could be undermined from within, reforms were either humane and neutral or simply conservative, reinforcing the system under the banner of progress. RAP had a long term radical goal but no means of achieving it. Like the visionary socialist with no time for 'reformism' RAP had to wait for the revolution to somehow happen; in this case for the collapse of the prison system under the weight of some as yet unforeseeable crisis. Paralysis was averted once RAP realised that by pressing for negative reforms the crisis could be precipitated by action. This seems straightforward, but in reality RAP's strategy was complicated by its commitment to alternatives.

RAP's intention was to research alternatives to prison, to demonstrate to the Home Office that many offenders, if not all, could be more effectively managed in community-based alternatives than in prison. Once the Home Office was convinced it would begin to switch its resources away from the prison system which would eventually wither and die. Further, when RAP spoke of researching alternatives it did not simply mean that it would find out about existing alternatives such as the Vera Bail project, and draw them to the attention of the Home Office, RAP wanted to set up its own alternatives to demonstrate through its own efforts that prisons were an unnecessary evil. This strategy was to cause a number of difficulties. In the first place there were practical problems and very soon the exhausting business of organising alternatives was openly questioned. Should RAP devote its energies to such activities or should its role be more political, persuading and educating rather than trying itself to demonstrate? As one activist was to write in what became an ongoing debate:

> For a long time now there has been some division of opinion in RAP about concrete 'alternatives', i.e. whether we should encourage people to start projects themselves and try to support them, or whether this was simply not our proper role. Perhaps Ros [Kane] 's thing in Newham [NAP] epitomises this difference, but this is merely the most ambitious one; there have been many earlier ones such as Excell House . . . I don't regard these myself

as divisive, although my own work is entirely political it has seemed to me that individuals or even groups of individuals with RAP's blessing might well do such work, but that it was tangential to RAP's main purpose and should never occupy much of our energies.[108]

This argument gained increasing force as time went by. RAP's membership in 1972 was over 600 and rising[109] but by 1975 it was probably well below 500. The bubble had burst, both in London and in the provinces where only Bristol and West Yorkshire branches appeared to be active. In this situation, and given that some members wanted RAP to put its energies into such things as exposing the 'true function' of the criminal law, it was inevitable that the idea of alternatives would seem less and less attractive. The struggle continues into 1977. The Newham Alternatives Project is still running even though RAP's official policy is now simply to demand abolition, it being the government's job to provide the alternatives. But the debate over 'concrete alternatives' was about more than simply the allocation of scarce resources, human or financial. In particular, the question was raised, had not RAP come to the conclusion in the spring of 1975 that alternative schemes 'within the present framework' were unacceptable, merely bulwarks to the existing social and political order? If this was so, then how could NAP survive, how could it operate within the present framework without becoming an instrument of repression in the service of an unequal society? Perhaps the best way to answer this would be to consider it in the context of RAP's attitude to Community Service Orders.

RAP had opposed Community Service Orders on three grounds. First, they were punitive, clearly intending to deprive offenders of their leisure time, and if they refused to cooperate the 'big stick' was ready in the background. Second, they were retributive: that offenders should repay their debt to the community was central to the whole idea of the new orders. Finally they were integrative so that the offender, instead of being educated to see himself as the victim of an unequal and corrupt society, was expected to work alongside voluntary workers whose wholesome influence would help him to integrate into the existing political order. All this was too much for RAP. Society's victims should not be punished or asked to repay their debts. Alternatives were only acceptable when they acknowledged this, and the only real justification for operating alternatives within the existing political order was if the offender/victim was helped to understand his oppression. How did NAP match up to these conditions? The short answer is not very well. The punitive edge of the deferred sentence was clearly demonstrated during NAP's first two year period. Of those who got a deferred sentence to NAP four were sent to prison or borstal at the end of their deferment, and another six were given fines.[110] On the question of retribution, the Home Office *Guide for the Courts* in 1972 specifically mentioned deferment in connection with reparation by the offender.[111] Finally, there is very little evidence that NAP managed much in the way of political education.

Integration, or in the language of treatment, rehabilitation, like punishment and retribution are central to the penal system. Any alternative which does not negate these functions is not a genuine alternative. This is why RAP was right to challenge Community Service Orders, to warn us against Greeks bearing false gifts. The Home Office had taken RAP's emphasis on community alternatives and simply reversed its assumptions. To the extent to which alternatives do not challenge the assumptions on which the penal system rests then they are acceptable. This is the history of NAP. It has defined itself within the system and is now accorded official recognition. Indeed, after a cautious start when it was busy cutting through NAP's radical rhetoric the Home Office has now even agreed to offer the project government money, a grant from the Voluntary Service Unit.[112] RAP's experiment with the Newham Alternatives Project illustrates its whole strategic dilemma. It seeks in the short term to operate alternatives in a system which is based on assumptions which are in contra-distinction to its own. The dangers and dilemmas have been noted by Mathiesen:

> *The opponent of the prevailing order is therefore presented with the choice between specifying alternatives – and thereby coming very close to the prevailing order in what he suggests – or emphasising completely different values – and thereby being rejected as irresponsible and unrealistic.* The choice is difficult, and many chose the former solution.
>
> It is, however, the more dangerous solution . . . Despite the difficulties connected with it, the latter solution must be the right one if you, initially, either disagree with one or more of the goals of the prevailing order, or give priority to goals which are in conflict with the prevailing ones. If you do not, in one of these ways, disagree with regard to goals, the question is a different one. But if you disagree, the right thing must be to stand on your no, and on the other values, and seek to communicate the values to groups in society which may participate in fighting for them. The ridicule and pressure which you are then exposed to

> is of course great; ridicule and pressure are a means of obstructing the communication of values to potential allies. And not only is the ridicule and pressure there – the accusations of 'undermining' society, 'political extremism', etc., are also strong, because the new values necessarily presuppose – if they are to be put into effect – comprehensive changes over and above the specific political area (for example, the area of correctional and penal policy) which constituted your point of departure. In other words, the choice easily becomes one between specifying 'alternatives' which in reality are very close to the prevailing order, and facing attempts from the establishment at 'defining you out' . . . .[113]

That RAP is confronted by this dilemma across the whole range of its activities is obvious enough. To the extent that it is not challenging the assumptions of the penal system, to the extent that it is prepared to operate NAP or for that matter draw up its annual survey showing how the rates of imprisonment in magistrates courts vary from place to place, then the Home Office will always be willing to enter into a 'constructive' dialogue. But if RAP goes beyond this, if it reveals its political edge then it is effectively 'defined out'.

Having considered the case against the Newham Alternatives Project it is extremely important to understand why, given RAP's radical outlook, it was ever allowed to get started in the first place. There are several obvious reasons. Christian Action was very much in favour of NAP because, as already suggested, it would satisfy the Charity Commissioners. RAP would be seen to be doing good works. Also, Christian Action was entitled in theory, at least, to 12½ per cent of any grants which might be raised to finance NAP. More significant though was RAP's loose structure with no desire or mechanism to stop any of its members from starting an alternative project if they wished. It should be emphasised, too, that the will to do something practical, something humanitarian was very strong. This was particularly so in the early days when RAP attracted a number of ex-prisoners. This should not be construed as being entirely naive. Ros Kane, for example, who pioneered NAP was prepared to admit that when it came to organising alternatives within the present system she might later come to realise that she was the victim of an illusion. [114] These reasons apart, NAP's main support rested on the simple but crucial fact that by no means all of RAP's members were anything like as radical as its rhetoric implied. For example, to have suggested that NAP was unacceptable because it did not challenge the assumptions on which the penal system was built would not have impressed everyone by a long way for not everyone in RAP was looking for 'genuine alternatives'. For the less radical an alternative was acceptable even if it served the same functions as imprisonment. The only condition it had to meet was that it avoided incarceration. An evaluation of alternatives was never made on the basis of whether or not they were retributive or whether they were designed to integrate the offender back into a corrupt and unequal society, to be passively controlled and exploited by either 'the powerful' or 'the ruling class'. In other words, RAP's so called moderates did not interpret the criminal law like radical pluralists, still less like Marxists. That this diverse political commitment led to difficulties is clear. As Duncan Leys was to comment in July 1974:

> There is a tendency for political and 'pressure' groups to wax and wane in membership and enthusiasm, according to all sorts of heterogeneous considerations, and this is especially true when the basis of cooperation is rather broad. RAP included in its early days people with very different ideas about the definition and origin of 'crime'. its political importance, etc. There were people whose impulses were almost wholly samaritan, and who did not question the sort of assumptions which are made by establishment figures about individual personal responsibility, with its corollaries of such concepts as 'rehabilitation', 'punishment', 'protection of society', but who were only moved by their appreciation of the inhumanity and degradation of prison. They were dissatisfied with existing organisations for 'penal reform', including the Howard League, with its timidity and establishment profile. There were others whose energies could only be usefully directed into channels which they envisaged as offering direct help to the victims of the prison system. For a time it seemed that people with these rather heterogeneous ideas could usefully work together, but one could no doubt have prophesied that this would not continue, and indeed the membership did include some people of the greatest political naivety.[115]

This is an interesting statement for a number of reasons, not least because it was made by someone with a developing interest in materialist criminology and an awareness of the divisions which were becoming apparent in the National Deviancy Conference.[116] However, more to the immediate point, it suggests that RAP developed from being a highly heterogeneous group to a smaller and more obviously radical group between 1970 and 1974. It clearly implies too that this was an almost inevitable development, as RAP's political edge became more radical so those members with a purely humanitarian interest were forced out since they suddenly realised that they were on the wrong bus. Although it is very difficult to substantiate this analysis, (the reasons why people left have not been recorded) it is difficult not to believe that Leys is on the right track. RAP did become more radical and this no doubt cost it members. To this extent, then, there is no disagreement with Leys. However, it would be quite wrong to infer from his analysis that those people with a non-political perspective opted out altogether in 1974, that RAP was somehow reduced to the radical left. This was simply not so for there were plenty of members still around with an essentially samaritan interest and it was this interest that gave NAP its support. One further point in Ley's analysis is of interest, namely, he not only suggests that the disenchantment of the 'samaritans' or 'politically naive' was inevitable, but also that from a radical point of view, it was desirable. There were plenty who would have agreed with him; more than one radical found RAP's ambivalence intolerable and left. However, whether this purity amounts to a strategic advantage is surely a matter for debate. Experience has shown that the more overt RAP's political message the more it is defined out. The fact that it has, in the language of politics, reformist elements is perhaps the only reason that it has been listened to at all. The politics of ambiguity might therefore be the only available tactic for a radical pressure group which wants to operate within the existing political system. There are many dangers, but what are the alternatives?

NOTES

[1] Gordon Rose, *The Struggle for Penal Reform,* Stevens, London, 1961, p.306.
[2] *Royal Commission on the Penal System in England and Wales,* HMSO, London, 1967, pp.33–53.
[3] RAP, *Annual Report,* 1971–72, p.1.
[4] As Ros Kane was later to explain on RAP's behalf, 'Our first meeting merged with the last meeting of the PRC. This was symbolic. New ideals were emerging, and a new confidence that they could find expression in reality. More comfortable prison conditions, we felt, would certainly be more humane, but just as we felt that prison was an irrelevant concept, so a campaign for better conditions would also be irrelevant'. *Christian Action Journal,* Summer 1972, p.3.
[5] See for example, RAP General Meeting, January 1972.

[6] Letter to Nick Mullen, 12 December 1970.
[7] The two salaries were to be divided between a full time office administrator and two part time workers, one concerned with campaigning and some research, the other with the coordination of practical projects. RAP General Meeting, February 1972.
[8] *Memorandum on RAP and Christian Action,* Christian Action, undated.
[9] It is interesting to note at this point that the sharp edge of RAP's radicalism was not lost on Hugh Klare who in a generous letter to Canon Collins supporting RAP's application to become a trial Christian Action project praised Sandra Roszkowski and Ros Kane but made it clear that he could not agree with their politics (1 January 1970).
[10] *House of Commons Debates,* vol.775, cols.306–8.
[11] D.E.R. Faulkner, 'The redevelopment of Holloway prison', *Howard Journal of Penology and Crime Prevention,* vol.13, no.3, pp. 122–132.
[12] D.E.R. Faulkner, 'The redevelopment of Holloway prison', *Howard Journal of Penology and Crime Prevention,* vol.13, no.3, p. 128.
[13] D.E.R. Faulkner, 'The redevelopment of Holloway prison', *Howard Journal of Penology and Crime Prevention,* vol.13, no.3, p. 129.
[14] D.E.R. Faulkner, 'The redevelopment of Holloway prison', *Howard Journal of Penology and Crime Prevention,* vol.13, no.3, p. 131.
[15] D.E.R. Faulkner, 'The redevelopment of Holloway prison', *Howard Journal of Penology and Crime Prevention,* vol.13, no.3, pp. 131–2.
[16] Katrin Fitzherbert, 'New Holloway?', *New Society,* 25 February 1971, pp.301–2.
[17] *RAP Newsletter,* no.2, January 1972.
[18] *RAP Newsletter,* no.3, January 1972.
[19] *Alternatives to Holloway,* (RAP),1972, pp.9–10.
[20] *Alternatives to Holloway,* (RAP),1972, pp.11–12.
[21] *Alternatives to Holloway,* (RAP),1972, pp.17–19.
[22] *Alternatives to Holloway,* (RAP),1972, p.18.
[23] For details of the Vera Bail Project see p.57.
[24] *Alternatives to Holloway,* (RAP),1972, p.22.
[25] *Alternatives to Holloway,* (RAP),1972, pp.48–9.
[26] *The Guardian,* 22 May 1972.
[27] *RAP Annual Report,* 1972, pp.5–6. It should be noted that not everyone in RAP was in favour of a rally; the idea, it seems, had been

pushed by Christian Action.
[28] *RAP Annual Report,* 1972, pp.4–5.
[29] Holloway Campaign Committee letter, 23 February 1972.
[30] *Alternatives to Holloway,* (RAP), 1972, p.32.
[31] *Prison Service Journal,* new series, no.8, October 1972, p.8.
[32] *RAP Newsletter,* vol.2, no.7, June 1973.
[33] *Working Party on Vagrancy and Street Offences Working Paper,* part II, HMSO, London, 1974.
[34] *'RAP On Street Offences', A criticism of the Working Paper of the Working Party on Vagrancy and Street Offences,* section III, RAP, March 1975.
[35] *'RAP On Street Offences', A criticism of the Working Paper of the Working Party on Vagrancy and Street Offences,* section I, RAP, March 1975.
[36] *RAP Newsletter,* November 1975.
[37] *RAP Newsletter,* November 1975.
[38] *RAP Newsletter,* January 1976.
[39] *House of Commons Debates,* vol.918, col.522.
[40] *New Society,* 13 December 1973.
[41] *New Society,* September 1972. For the best account of PROP, see Mike Fitzgerald, *Prisoners in Revolt,* Penguin, Harmondsworth, 1977.
[42] *RAP Newsletter,* September/October 1972.
[43] RAP Nucleus Meeting, 14 January 1974.
[44] *Non-Custodial and Semi-Custodial Penalties, Report of the Advisory Council on the Penal System,* HMSO, 1970.
[45] *Non-Custodial and Semi-Custodial Penalties, Report of the Advisory Council on the Penal System,* HMSO, 1970, para 31.
[46] *Non-Custodial and Semi-Custodial Penalties, Report of the Advisory Council on the Penal System,* HMSO, 1970, para 35.
[47] *Non-Custodial and Semi-Custodial Penalties, Report of the Advisory Council on the Penal System,* HMSO, 1970, paras. 61 and 63.
[48] *Home Office Working Group on Community Service by Offenders:* Report, para 7.
[49] *Home Office Working Group on Community Service by Offenders:* Report, para 7.
[50] *Community Service Orders,* Home Office Research Unit, HMSO, London, 1975.
[51] *Community Service Orders,* Home Office Research Unit, HMSO, 1975.
[52] Later published as *Community Service Orders in Inner London: An Exercise in Illusion,* RAP, Spring 1973.

[53] *Community Service by Offenders,* Inner London Probation and After-care Service, 1975, pp.3, 4, 5.
[54] *RAP Newsletter,* March 1975.
[55] *RAP Newsletter,* June 1975.
[56] *RAP Newsletter,* vol.3, no.3 (undated).
[57] *PROBE,* no.1, pp.16–17, Napo Members Action Group, undated.
[58] *RAP Newsletter,* June 1974.
[59] *RAP Newsletter,* September 1974.
[60] *NAPO Newsletter,* August 1974.
[61] *RAP Newsletter,* September 1974.
[62] Letter from Mr Kenneth Howe, *NAPO Newsletter,* August 1975.
[63] *PROBE,* no.4, May 1975, p.9.
[64] *Probation Journal,* vol.22, no.3, 1975, p.70.
[65] Benedict Nightingale, *Charities,* Allen Lane, London, 1973, p.49.
[66] *Charity Law – only a new start will do,* The Charity Law Reform Committee, p.4.
[67] *Christian Action Journal,* Christian Action, London, Summer 1972, pp.10–11.
[68] *Christian Action Journal,* Christian Action, London, Winter 1972–73, p.2.
[69] *RAP Newsletter,* January 1972.
[70] Excell House Community Project, broadsheet by M. Shields, (undated).
[71] *Newham Alternatives Project,* RAP, London, 1976, p.4.
[72] Letter from Ros Kane to the Home Office, 11 November 1973.
[73] *Newham Alternatives Project,* RAP, London, 1976, pp.11–14.
[74] *Newham Alternatives Project,* RAP, London, 1976, pp.16–23.
[75] *Newham Alternatives Project,* RAP, London, 1976, p.13.
[76] *Newham Alternatives Project,* RAP, London, 1976, p.14.
[77] *Newham Recorder,* 1 August 1974.
[78] *Newham Alternatives Project,* RAP, London, 1976, p.15.
[79] *Newham Alternatives Project,* RAP, London, 1976, p.42.
[80] *The Guardian,* 8 December 1975, p.6.
[81] *The Guardian,* 29 April 1975, p.16.
[82] Memorandum by Radical Alternatives to Prison on the Children and Young Persons Act, 1969, and the implications of some of its provisions, submitted to the Social Services Subcommittee of the Expenditure Committee of the House of Commons, September 1974, para 2.
[83] This does not mean that RAP's evidence to the Social Services Subcommittee was only concerned with 'bread and butter' issues. On the contrary, it referred to what many commentators regarded as a

central contradiction in the Act, its function to care for the child and yet at the same time protect society (para 3). However, to the extent that the memorandum addressed itself to the 1969 Act and its consequences it did not develop its wider political critique of children in trouble.

[84] *Children Out of Trouble*, RAP, London, Spring 1974, p.6.
[85] *Children Out of Trouble*, RAP, London, Spring 1974, p.5.
[86] *New Society*, 18 April 1974, p.120.
[87] *Prison Officers Magazine*, vol.63 (7), p.197.
[88] *Prison Officers Magazine*, vol.63 (7), p.200.
[89] *Prison Officers Magazine*, vol.63 (7), p.200.
[90] *House of Commons Debates*, vol.856, cols.215 and 216.
[91] *House of Commons Debates*, vol.867/868, col.42.
[92] *House of Commons Debates*, vol.877, col.492.
[93] *The Sunday Times*, 6 October 1974.
[94] *Summary of Public Meeting on Control Units*, 28 November 1974, RAP, London, p.3.
[95] *RAP Newsletter*, vol.3, no.10, November 1974, p.2.
[96] For the crumbling alliance see *RAP Nucleus Minutes*, 19 March 1975, para 4. NCCL tried to reinstate the Howard League.
[97] Pamphlet announcing the 28 November Public Meeting on Control Units, RAP, London, p.3.
[98] *House of Commons Debates*, vol.898, cols.283/284.
[99] *The Guardian*, 6 June 1975.
[100] *RAP Newsletter*, June 1976, p.3.
[101] HLPR, *Annual Report*, 1974–75, p.5.
[102] For some frightening possibilities see Mike Fitzgerald, *Control Units and The Shape of Things to Come*, RAP, London, 1975.
[103] *RAP Newsletter*, undated, probably Autumn 1972.
[104] *RAP Newsletter*, vol.1, no.10, September/October 1972.
[105] T. Mathiesen, *The Politics of Abolition*, Martin Robertson, London, 1974, chapter 7. Mathiesen was directly involved with pressure groups in the field of criminal policy in Scandinavia. As early as 1973 RAP invited the Danish group KRIM to visit London to exchange ideas (Correspondence KRIM/RAP October 1973). Individual members seem to have been reasonably well informed about KRIM prior to this official invitation (*RAP Newsletter*, June 1973).
[106] Some of RAP's full time workers have argued, in private correspondence, that reforms which could bring down the prison system were being discussed before 1975. However, there was no systematic exposition of a strategy along these lines.
[107] T. Mathiesen, *The Politics of Abolition*, Martin Robertson,

London, p.203.
[108] A memorandum for discussion at a RAP Nucleus Meeting, undated, probably June 1974.
[109] *RAP Annual Report,* 1972, p.1.
[110] *Newham Alternatives Project,* RAP, London, 1976, p.42.
[111] *Newham Alternatives Project,* RAP, London, 1976, p.3.
[112] *RAP Newsletter,* March 1977, p.2.
[113] T. Mathiesen, *The Politics of Abolition,* Martin Robertson, London, pp.85–6.
[114] *RAP Newsletter,* vol.3, no.3.
[115] A memorandum for discussion at a RAP Nucleus Meeting, July 1974.
[116] Duncan Leys' review of *Critical Criminology* (edited by Taylor, Walton and Young, 1975) demonstrates this interest very clearly. He wrote, in the course of that review: 'It became obvious at the National Deviancy Conference at Cardiff this year that the active membership was divided over what should be the future and main thrust of radical criminology. The concept of materialist criminology lies at the heart of this division, namely the acceptance of class domination, inherent in capitalism (including state capitalism) as the basis of a discriminatory and grossly biased system of law. This leads to the conclusion, at which many have no doubt arrived without direct acknowledgement to Karl Marx, that the present legal system, the ideology of the police, courts and prisons, form the basis of political power. Criminology, social institutions and politics are, in this reading, inseparable, and any supposed objectivity . . . of sociological work an illusion.' (*RAP Newsletter*, November 1975, p.2)

6 Conclusion

In 1966 The Howard League for Penal Reform had been in business, in one form or another, for a hundred years. To mark its centenary the League published a collection of essays with a foreword by its Chairman, the late Sir Kenneth Younger.[1] Looking back over the League's long and distinguished history Sir Kenneth argued that its main function had been to goad and to criticise, to demand that reforms should come faster and go further. Almost inevitably this had led the League into conflict with those who operated the levers of power. However, and this was the Chairman's main point, such conflict had not prevented the growth of a sense of partnership between the League and successive Home Secretaries and their civil servants. This observation is indeed true. From William Tallack, through Margery Fry to Hugh Klare, the partnership was sustained and there is no doubt, from the League's point of view at least, that it brought many benefits. However, it would be foolish to ignore the fact that such a close relationship has, on occasions, turned out to be inward-looking and conservative, unable to accommodate new ideas at the expense of old assumptions. This was surely so in the late 1960s and early 1970s. The League's principal focus was the prison system and its links with those civil servants who ran the system were so close that their concerns became the League's concerns. Locked as it was in the struggle to make the prison system somehow more efficient and humane, the League lost out to other groups in the penal lobby who stressed the need for community-based alternatives to incarceration. The penal debate had entirely altered its terms of reference and the League had to work hard to catch up with the frontrunners like Radical Alternatives to Prison. The validity of this general analysis is in no way undermined by the knowledge that certain prominent individuals associated with the League, for instance, Louis Blom-Cooper who served on the Wootton Committee, were receptive to the new emphasis on alternatives.

To some extent the Howard League's partnership, as Sir Kenneth Younger refers to it, with Home Secretaries and their civil servants is not now as firm in respect of the prison system as it was. In the inter-war period the relationship between ruling elites was easy and familiar and Margery Fry conducted her dialogue with the Prison Commissioners, notably Maurice Waller, very much on a personal basis.[2] Hugh Klare was inclined to operate along similar lines believing that prison reform was not popular with the public and therefore the best tactic was to persuade progressive Commissioners like Sir Lionel Fox, and reforms would then follow.[3] With the demise of the Prison Commission this pattern of influence has slowly declined. The contacts built up by Klare under the old regime have been far less secure since his departure, and with the new Prison Department firmly in the womb of the Home Office getting changes in the prison system is not quite so easy or so direct. This may not be a bad thing if it pushes the League's concerns wider.

It would be wrong, however, to believe that the demise of the old Prison Commission with its relatively stable membership has somehow left the Howard League out in the cold. This is clearly not so since it can get access to Holloway, inspect the fearful control units and in association with Justice and NACRO it was given official permission to circularise the mysterious Boards of Visitors.[4] The rewards for 'responsible' and 'cooperative' groups are various. The League's caution, appearing to verge on ambivalence over control units does not mean that these rewards have been suitably paid for, that the League is returning to a position of compromise and almost total inhibition in its dealings with those who operate the penal system. This is possible, of course, but it seems unlikely. In the wake of the Birmingham pub bombing incident, for example, when IRA prisoners were allegedly assaulted the League called for a full and open enquiry; and when PROP called on Islington Council to concern itself more with what was going on inside Holloway and Pentonville the League gave PROP its full support.[5] No doubt radicals will regard such public commitments with suspicion, remembering in particular how the Howard League effectively undermined PROP's prison protests in 1972 by claiming that they were likely to lead to a hardening of attitudes against reform and therefore ought to be abandoned. However, to take up such a position is perhaps to miss the point, which is that relatively the League seems to have taken up a more critical position *vis-a-vis* the Prison Department than in the past and this at least is to be welcomed. In this context the League's complaint is that one of the weaknesses of the present Prison Department is that it suffers from the civil service tradition of switching its senior administrators from department to department so that the official the League has become used to dealing with suddenly turns into someone else. But this complaint should be turned on its head and seen as an advantage since it makes the League less personally committed and, as a consequence, more free to criticise. The fact that between 1964 and 1973 there have been no less than five chairmen of the Prison Board may be better for the League than it is sometimes prepared to admit.[6]

On wider issues of penal policy it hardly needs restating that the decision making environment in which the League now operates is more complex than in the past. The Home Office is now surrounded by so many permanent and *ad hoc* advisory committees that on any given policy it is becoming increasingly difficult to say exactly what influences were decisive in helping to persuade the Home Secretary, and his advisors, to adopt one line rather than another. The League had to adapt to this environment, and if its partnership with successive Home Secretaries and their civil servants became less direct than in the past, it continued to make a meaningful contribution through the work of individuals like Sir George Benson, Sir Kenneth Younger and Louis Blom-Cooper whose services on official committees the government has always been anxious to enlist. Of course, the League's contribution is just one of many contributions; the penal lobby is crowded in the 1970s and it is worth considering how the Howard League sees itself in relation to other groups, in particular, NACRO, PROP and RAP.

NACRO, which was founded to replace the National Association for Discharged Prisoners Aid Societies, was originally given very wide terms of reference which included the prevention of crime and the training of wardens to run hostels for discharged prisoners. In recent years, and particularly under the leadership of Nicholas Hinton, NACRO has devoted a lot of its energies to demonstration projects, projects which are aimed not simply at providing after-care, but which are intended to show that for many offenders prison is unnecessary, and that viable and constructive alternatives can be made available. NACRO's work made sense to Martin Wright, the Howard League's Director. People need to be shown that there are alternatives to prison which not only work, but which can also benefit the wider community. A government funded organisation like NACRO with the freedom to experiment is well suited to demonstrate what can be achieved.[7]

Martin Wright also sees PROP as having a very real place in the penal lobby. As a pressure group of prisoners and ex-prisoners it knows where the shoe pinches, which is more than can be said of many other groups. Clearly, Wright has doubts and anxieties about PROP's militant potential, but he is at least willing to accept that the prison system's 'clients' should be heard. He also believes that RAP has a legitimate place in the struggle and in an article which completely ignored its radical politics he gave full praise to the group for its achievement in returning to fundamentals, its audacity in asking the question, why do we need to imprison people at all? [8] Wright values

RAP as a fundamentalist group, believing that there is a real need in the penal lobby for a tough-minded group which is more interested in ideals than 'the art of the possible' and which is under no obligation to use the usual polite channels of protest when it believes that civil servants at the Home Office or their political masters are failing in their duty. This does not mean that Wright is impressed by all that RAP has done. On the contrary, he believes that some of its schemes have been wholly impracticable while some of its arguments cannot escape the charge of 'oversimplification'.[9] Equally important is that uncompromising idealism in the penal lobby can easily reinforce the old prejudice that reforming pressure groups like RAP are somehow 'soft' on criminals while ignoring their unfortunate victims. The balance to be struck is a delicate one and RAP should bear this in mind.

But how does the Howard League stand in relation to these other groups? For Wright at least the answer is clear. While there is undoubtedly the need for a pressure group to demonstrate alternatives (NACRO), another to represent the clients (PROP) and a third to stress fundamentals (RAP), there remains the need for

> a think-tank, independent not only of the government but of the exigencies of day to day management of projects, but including practitioners among its members and maintaining informal links with ministers and civil servants to ensure that its proposals and criticisms are reasonably well informed.[10]

This is the role of the Howard League, and its campaign for an information centre on crime reflects this; it is the search for data to feed into its think-tank where practitioners and experts will together assess its relevance for government. Wright's conceptualisation of the penal lobby breaks down in practice, as he is the first to admit. NACRO, for example, has joined the League's think-tank on more than one occasion, and this has been welcomed since Martin Wright in particular is anxious that all pressure groups in the penal lobby should cooperate, a united front on occasions being the best way forward, and the debacle over control units not seen as a barrier to any further cooperation. To some extent Wright laboured cooperation, anxious no doubt to counter any suggestion that the League was unwilling or somehow unable to work with more radical groups because of its links with the Home Office. These links were not denied, nor was it denied that in sometimes receiving confidential information the League must, to some extent at least, be compromised. This after all was why

Wright could see a role for a group like RAP, why he felt its presence in the penal lobby was important. What he was reacting against was any suggestion that the Howard League was so plugged into the political system that its capacity to cooperate with other more radical groups was always nil.

It seems probably, though not certain, that this analysis of the penal lobby would have appealed to a number of RAP's members. For those who joined RAP to campaign against prisons, and who did so with little or no awareness of the political context of that campaign, the Howard League's stress on cooperation must have seemed sensible, particularly if RAP defined its cooperation on the basis of the distinction between positive and negative reforms. For others though, even if cooperation was not ruled out, Wright's analysis simply obscured the Howard League's highly political role. That is, for Marxists and radical pluralists the criminal law is, in the one case, in the service of the ruling class, in the other, in the service of powerful groups; and to the extent that the Howard League works to reform or rehabilitate those who are labelled as criminals then it is clearly and demonstrably acting in the interests of the ruling class or powerful groups and this is how it achieved the status of a second world pressure group.

RAP's view of the Howard League as an establishment pressure group has been made public on more than one occasion. In reply to the League's embarrassment over the control units issue, for example, RAP commented:

> There is here an absolutely fundamental difference in attitude . . . Briefly, the Howard League is an 'approved group' because it threatens nothing; its council and its membership are to a man within the sacred fold of the establishment; its posture is vaguely samaritan, but infinitely cautious; it believes in 'human rights' but it is not prepared to challenge the Home Office on the penal system wholeheartedly.
>
> It subscribes to the idea of rehabilitation; there is no, and will be no, interpretation of the penal system and prison as a political structure at the very heart of political power; and it is wonderful how the perception of this truth can blow your mind. [11]

This judgement offered no real hope of a lasting compromise, but as already indicated, not everyone in RAP felt like this. There were, in fact, clear differences between the radical and politically conscious and those members whose political perspective was, to put it mildly, underdeveloped. These differences were evident not only in London but also in the provinces. At Bradford, for example, there was genuine uncertainty about what was implied by the label, radical.[12] Much the same problem arose in Manchester where some members, 'Found much objection to the word "radical"'.[13] At Bristol too, perhaps RAP's most active and successful regional group, 'We continually find there is a need to thrash out differences of opinion and of philosophy. We have our own internal bickering often over differing political views.'[14] These uncertainties and differences were held partly to blame for RAP's state of crisis in the winter of 1975–76.

At a national emergency meeting in February 1976 it was revealed that RAP had been operating for five months without its central committee, the Nucleus. By 1976 also the relationship between Christian Action and RAP had reached a very low ebb and Christian Action had set up its own subcommittee to consider what action should be taken in the immediate future.[15]

Although the national emergency meeting did not resolve RAP's political ambiguities – it could never have done that – it did at least make two important decisions. The first was that RAP should continue in existence. The second was that a policy committee should be formed to be responsible for RAP's two full time workers, for liaison with regional groups and Christian Action and, finally, for considering alternative ways of raising revenue.[16] The decision that RAP should continue was hardly surprising. Its early and valuable contribution to the campaign for alternatives is widely accepted, and there is no evidence that the campaign is by any means over. For radicals, of course, this may be an ironic conclusion since the alternatives so far provided have been, in their terms at least, far from radical. That the policy committee could have a crucial role to play in RAP's future is obvious; it should not only help to provide more coherence, it might also encourage a wider structure of study groups. Such a structure is badly needed, RAP's contribution to the ongoing debate on penal policy is, at the present time, hardly visible. Of course to expect the policy committee to achieve total coherence is asking too much. RAP is far too heterogeneous a pressure group to ever guarantee that its members will pull together in the same direction for long. The present state of the 'factions' seems to indicate a shift to the right. For NAP to have accepted government money was a decisive (logical?) step. Further, the project is now to be guided onto 'firmer ground' by a management/advisory committee which includes as one of its members none other than Martin Wright from the Howard League. For some time now Christian Action has been inclined to 'clear' RAP's activities with the Howard League and in the light of this Wright's appointment is not unexpected: it simply formalises an existing link.[17] For radicals, this apparent shift to the right, even allowing for the politics of ambiguity, might turn out to be more than they are prepared to tolerate. On the other hand, some RAP members will find the shift much to their liking, arguing that the group's radical rhetoric, bordering as it sometimes does on crude determinism and an oversimplified interpretation of criminal law, is unrepresentative of majority opinion and has already done more than enough to distort RAP's image.

Whether or not RAP's rhetoric makes for such a distortion of what its members really believe is difficult to determine but it is clear that its public statements have been interpreted by successive Home Secretaries and their civil servants as containing a message that is foreign and ideologically hostile. True, the message has not always been that well formed, sometimes it has been frankly ambiguous, but it is this very ambiguity, this apparent willingness to compromise with the existing system by operating projects like NAP, that has given RAP at least some legitimacy in the pressure group universe. Of course, even that legitimacy is challenged, and the access that it offers, limited. That second world groups are much more privileged was perfectly illustrated by Home Secretary Roy Jenkins when in reply to a Parliamentary Question he accepted that whereas there were 'frequent' contacts between his department and the Howard League his civil servants only met RAP 'from time to time'.[18] This disadvantageous position need not always apply. RAP can drop its radical framework and make the transition from the third to the second world. Alternatively it can drop out of the pressure group universe altogether, resolve its ambiguities in an even more radical direction and move into what Benewick suggests is a fourth world, the world of the expelled. Both possibilities are open to RAP, both tendencies are visible.

To conceive of politics as a play-off between rival groups for marginal gain presupposes an ideological consensus. It is not our contention that no such ideological consensus exists in Britain at the present time, clearly it does, though perhaps less securely than in the past, and more contentious, it may even be argued that it is little more than the conformity induced by long standing hegemonic domination. But it is certain that any group which challenges the consensus, to the extent that it offers an explicit ideological alternative is defined out, and becomes a dissident minority. Liberals may claim that at least western democracies 'define out' such minority groups far less ruthlessly than totalitarian regimes. This may be so, but the ideological limits of that tolerance should not be obscured.

NOTES

[1] H. Klare (ed.), *Changing Concepts of Crime and its Treatment*, Pergamon, London, 1966.
[2] Margery Fry's book, *Arms of the Law*, Gollancz, London, 1951, is dedicated to the memory of Maurice Waller.
[3] Martin Wright, 'Tactics of reform' in Sean McConville (ed.), *The Use of Imprisonment*, Routledge and Kegan Paul, London, 1975.
[4] For the full extent of the Prison Department's cooperation see *Boards of Visitors of Penal Institutions*, Justice, Howard League and NACRO, London, 1975, pp.8–9.
[5] HLPR *Annual Report*, 1975–76, p.6. HLPR *Newsletter*, Summer 1976, p.1.
[6] Martin Wright, 'Tactics of reform' in Sean McConville (ed.), *The Use of Imprisonment*, Routledge and Kegan Paul, London, 1975, p.92.
[7] Martin Wright, 'Tactics of reform' in Sean McConville (ed.), *The Use of Imprisonment*, Routledge and Kegan Paul, London, 1975, pp. 96–7.
[8] Martin Wright, 'Tactics of reform' in Sean McConville (ed.), *The Use of Imprisonment*, Routledge and Kegan Paul, London, 1975, p. 93.
[9] Martin Wright, 'Tactics of reform' in Sean McConville (ed.), *The Use of Imprisonment*, Routledge and Kegan Paul, London, 1975, p. 93.
[10] Martin Wright, 'Tactics of reform' in Sean McConville (ed.), *The Use of Imprisonment*, Routledge and Kegan Paul, London, 1975, p. 97.
[11] RAP *Newsletter*, January 1976.
[12] Minutes, Radical Alternatives to Prison, Bradford Group, 28 April 1974, para 4.
[13] Report of National RAP meeting 7–8 April 1973, p.1.
[14] Report from Bristol RAP, October 1972 – December 1973, p.3.
[15] Report of National RAP meeting, March 1976, p.1.
[16] Report of National RAP meeting, March 1976, p.2.
[17] Christian Action's tendency to refer, if in doubt, to Martin Wright for an opinion on RAP's activities was particularly resented by Gail Coles and Elizabeth Middleton, RAP's two full time workers.
[18] *House of Commons Debates*, vol.896/897, col.207.

Select Bibliography

Barnett, M.J., *The Politics of Legislation,* Weidenfeld and Nicolson, London, 1969.

Baskin, D., *American Pluralist Democracy: A Critique,* Van Nostrand, London, 1971.

Becker, H., *Outsiders,* Free Press, New York, 1963.

Beer, S., *Modern British Politics,* Faber and Faber, London, 1965.

Benewick, R., Berki, R.N. and Parekh, Bhikhu (eds), *Knowledge and Belief in Politics,* Allen and Unwin, London, 1963.

Bentley, A.F., *The Process of Government,* University of Chicago Press, 1908.

Christoph, J., *Capital Punishment and British Politics,* Allen and Unwin, London, 1962.

Cohen, S. and Taylor, L., *Psychological Survival,* Penguin, Harmondsworth, 1972.

Crick, B. (ed.), *Essays on Reform,* Oxford University Press, London, 1967.

Crick, B., *In Defence of Politics,* Penguin, Harmondsworth, 1964.

Crick, B., *The American Science of Politics,* Routledge and Kegan Paul, London, 1959.

Dahl, R., *A Preface to Democratic Theory,* University of Chicago Press, Chicago, 1956.

Finer, S., *Anonymous Empire,* Pall Mall Press, London, 1958.

Fitzgerald, M., *Prisoners in Revolt,* Penguin, Harmondsworth, 1977.

Fry, M., *Arms of the Law,* Gollancz, London, 1951.

Hood, R. (ed.), *Crime, Criminology and Public Policy,* Heinemann, London, 1974.

Jones, E.H., *Margery Fry,* Oxford University Press, London, 1961.

Klare, H., *Changing Concepts of Crime and Its Treatment,* Pergamon, London, 1966.

Kornhauser, W., *The Politics of Mass Society,* Routledge and Kegan Paul, London, 1960.

Lipset, S.M., *Political Man,* Mercury Books, London, 1963.

Mathiesen, T., *The Politics of Abolition,* Martin Robertson, London, 1974.

Matza, D., *Becoming Deviant,* Prentice Hall, London, 1969.
Delinquency and Draft, John Wiley, New York, 1964.

McConville, S. (ed.), *The Use of Imprisonment,* Routledge and Kegan Paul, London, 1975.

Miliband, R., *The State in Capitalist Society,* Weidenfeld and Nicolson, London, 1969.
Nightingale, B., *Charities,* Allen Lane, London, 1973.
Pearce, F., *Crimes of the Powerful,* Pluto Press, London, 1976.
Rock, P. and McIntosh, M. (eds), *Deviance and Social Control,* Tavistock Publications, London, 1974.
Rose, G., *The Struggle for Penal Reform,* Stevens, London, 1961.
Self, P. and Storing, H., *The State and The Farmer,* Allen and Unwin, London, 1962.
Stewart, J.D., *British Pressure Groups,* Oxford University Press, London, 1958.
Taylor, I., Walton, P. and Young, J. (eds), *Critical Criminology,* Routledge and Kegan Paul, London, 1975.
Taylor, I., Walton, P. and Young, J., *The New Criminology,* Routledge and Kegan Paul, London, 1973.
Truman, D.B., *The Governmental Process,* Knopf, New York, 1951.
Walkland, S.A., *The Legislative Process in Great Britain,* Allen and Unwin, London, 1968.
Wiles, P. (ed.), *The Sociology of Crime and Delinquency in Britain, vol.2: The New Criminologies,* Martin Robertson, London, 1976.

Index

References from Notes indicated by 'n' after page reference.

Advisory Council on the Penal System 48, 58, 80
Advisory Council on the Treatment of Offenders (ACTO) 37, 45, 60, 88
After-care report 60
Alcoholics 105
Alternatives to Holloway 103–7 *passim*
American Political Science Review 10
Anti-Violence League (AVL) 49, 83

BBC 137
Bail 56, 57
Barber, Anthony 112
Barnett, M. Joel 18
Becker, Howard 93
Beer, Samuel 8, 11, 15, 24, 93
Benewick, Robert 22
Benson, George 34, 37, 43
Bentley, Arthur Fisher 6, 12
Blaisdell, Donald C. 7
Blake, George 53
Blom-Cooper, Louis 61
Blumberg, Myrna 81
British Medical Association, study of 13
Brockway, Fenner 32, 100
Buckingham, Helen 110
Butler, R.A. 43, 76
British Pressure Groups: their role in relation to the House of Commons 11

Cadbury Trust 127
Cambridge Institute of Criminology 45, 63, 75
Campaign for Nucleur Disarmament 99
Callaghan, James 77, 102
Capital punishment 38
Capital Punishment and British Politics 12
Capital Punishment in the 20th Century 38
Carr, Robert 112, 133, 137
Case Con 90
Charity Law Reform Committee 125
Central After-Care Association 59
Children 49, 50
Children and Young Persons Act 130
Children Out of Trouble 131
Childs, Harewood 7
Christian ACtion 4, 100, 124, 156
Christian Action Journal 125
Cohen Commission (1956) 20
Collins, Canon John 4
Committee of 100 99
Committee on Children and Young Persons 49
Community Service Orders 115–18 *passim*, 127, 141
Conservative Party 9, 20
Control Unit Action Group (CUAG) 133
Corporal punishment 33, 81
Crick, Bernard 7, 12, 15
Crime rate 36, 79, 127

Criminal Justices Act (1938) 34, 35, 37; (1947) 79; (1948) 59; (1960) 39, 42, 48, 49, 83; (1961) 80; (1972) 56, 117
Criminal Record Office 63
Custody and Control Order (CCO) 121, 122

Dahl, Robert 8
Daily Chronicle 29
Daily Herald 81
Dartmoor prison 32
Davies, Jean 126
Day Training Centres 55, 56
Departmental Committees: on Corporal Punishment 34; on Homosexuality and Prostitution 91; on Young Offenders 33
Detention centres 79, 80
Deviant behaviour 89, 90
Discharged Prisoners' Aid Societies 34, 59
Dixon, Piers 66

Eckstein, Harry 11, 88
Economic Power and Political Pressures (1941) 7

Family Committees and Family Courts 50
Faulks Committee on Defamation 65, 66
Female crime 104, 105, 108, 110
Finer, S.E. 11, 12, 19, 21
First Offenders Act (1958) 37, 75
Fisher Committee 49
Fitzherbert, Katherine 103
Forensic psychiatry 57
Fox, Sir Lionel 76, 152
Frankl, Mrs Kate 61
Fry, Margery 3, 31, 32, 42, 45, 50, 68, 75

Gardiner, Lord 61, 64, 114
Gibbens, T.C.N. 57
Gladstone Committee (1894) 29
Gollanz, Victor 39, 41
Granting Bail-Magistrates' Courts 106
Grünhut, Max 42, 83
Guardian 105, 130, 135

Heath, Edward 20, 106
Herring, Pendleton 7
Hoare, Sir Samuel 34
Hobhouse, Stephen 31
Hodge, Henry 61
Hodgetts, Colin 100
Holloway Prison 31, 102–4 *passim,* 131
Home Office 33, 127; ACTO 37; community-based correctives 2; Criminal Dept. 61; Prison Commission 87; Prison Dept. 51; Report on Murder (1957–68) 41; Research Unit 44, 63, 119; Statistical Advisor 43; Voluntary Service Unit 85; Wolfenden Committee 108
Homicide Act (1957) 40, 41
Hood, Roger 48
House of Commons 131
Howard Association 28–74 *see also* Howard League
Howard League for Penal Reform (HLPR) 2, 21: after-care 59; bail 56; capital punishment 39, 42; compensation to victims 68; CUAG 135; Development Officer 87; election of members 37; Holloway prison 107; Howard Centre for Penalogy 47;

Parliamentary Panel Reform Group 34; prison system 78; Rehabilitation of Offenders' Act 60; relationship with Home Office 24; 'Tactics of Reform' 84
Howe, Kenneth 122
Humanitarian League 29

Imprisonment 2
Ingleby, Viscount 49
Institute for the Study and Treatment of Delinquency (ISTD) 33, 42, 47, 108
Islington Council 152

Jenkins, Roy 48
Journal of Sociology 11
Justice 61, 68
Juvenile Courts 49
Juvenile delinquency 132

Kane, Ros 100
Kidlington detention centre 79
Klare, Hugh 45, 51, 52, 54
Koestler, Arthur 39
Kornhauser, W. 10, 11

Labour Party 8, 9, 31, 41, 49
Leeson, Cecil 32
Legal Aid, appeals 33
Leys, Duncan 144
Lloyd Jacobs Committee 20
Lloyd, Selwyn 20
Lodge, T.S. 43
Longford Committee 52
Longford, Lord 4, 80
Lyon, Alex 65, 66

McKenzie, W.J.M. 14, 121
Mackintosh, John 17
Magistrates 129, 143
Magistrates' Association 32, 67
Magistrates' courts 56, 57, 104
Manhattan Bail Project 104
Mannheim, Hermann 42
Marks, Kenneth 65, 66
Masterson, John 137
Matza, David 89, 93
Maxwell, Alexander 42
Mountbatten Report 54
Movement for the Preservation of the Rights of Prisoners (PROP) 79 *see also* PROP

National Association for the Care and Resettlement of Offenders (NACRO) 54
National Association of Probation Officers (NAPO) 121, 123
National Campaign for the Abolition of Capital Punishment 39, 41, 45
National Council for the Abolition of the Death Penalty 38
National Deviancy Conference (NDC) 88, 144
Newham Alternatives Project 126, 127, 128, 141
New Society 103, 112, 132

Observer 87
Offences 35, 36, 37, 105, 108
Offenders, rehabilitation of 60
Open prison 32
Organised Interests in British National Politics (1961) 11

Parliament 16, 20, 29, 32
Paterson, Sir Alexander 34
Patrick, Neil 121
Penal system 32, 44, 91
Pluralism 6–27
Poor Prisoners Defence Act (1930) 33, 75

Potter, A. 11, 21
Preservation of the Rights of Prisoners (PROP) 2, 112, 152
Prison: autonomy 28; children in 131; control units 133; Howard League memorandum 78; population 111; rebuilding programme 53; riots 111, 133; staff 52, 59, 78
Prison Commission 83, 87, 152
Prison Dept. 53, 102, 152
Prison Medical Reform Council (PMRC) 36, 76, 100
Prison Officers Association 114, 123, 133
Prison Service Journal 108
Prison Welfare Officers 59
Probation and After-care Service 120
Prostitution 108, 110
Prostitutes United for Social and Sexual Integration (PUSSI) 110

Radical Alternatives to Prison (RAP) 2, 24, 85, 90, 96; campaign against prison building 111; Children Out of Trouble 131; *Christian Action Journal* 125; deferred sentence 126; divisions within 143; manifesto 100; on prisons and alternatives 119; 'Political RAP' 125; young offenders 121; women in prison 102; *see also* Christian Action; Prison Medical Reform Council; PROP
Race Relations Act (1965) 20
Radzinowicz, Leon 43, 46, 92, 99
Radzinowicz Report 133
Rehabilitation 54, 60, 64, 109
Remands 104
Rose, Gordon 12, 28, 35, 86, 99
Roszkowski, Sandra 100
Royal Commissions: on Capital Punishment 39; on Penal Servitude (1879) 29; on the Penal System (1964) 46; on the Penal System (1965) 91, 99
Russell, Champion 32

St. John, Arthur 31
Scott, Dorothy 32
Select Committee on Capital Punishment 38
Self, P. 12, 21, 87
Sentences 56, 127, 130
Sieghart, Paul 61
Silverman, Sidney 39
Simon Community 105
Society for the Abolition of Capital Punishment 28
Soskice, Sir Frank 47
Stewart, J.D. 11, 21
Stoneham, Lord 80
Storing, H. 12, 21, 87
Streat, Sir Raymond 18
Street Offenders Act (1959) 109
Summary Jurisdiction (Appeals) Act (1933) 33, 75
Sunday Times 134
Supervision and Control Order 121

Tallack, William 28, 30
Templewood, Lord 36; *see also* Sir Samuel Hoare
Thorpe, David 131
Time Out 103
Tweedie, Jill 105

Vagrancy 108, 110
Vera Bail Project 57

Wilkins, Leslie 43
Withers, Sir John 33
Wolfenden Committee (1957) 108
Wootton, Lady 80
Wootton Report (1970) 115
Working Group on Community Service by Offenders 116
Working Party on Previous Convictions 61, 63
Working Party on Vagrancy and Street Offences 110
Wormwood Scrubbs 54
Wright, Martin 84
Women in prison 102; *see also* RAP

Yorkshire Post 110
Young Adult Offenders (1974) 58
Young Delinquent 42
Young, Jock 90, 93
Young Offender 33, 50, 57, 121
Younger Report 5, 121
Younger, Sir Kenneth 88, 151